T0271347

Economic Innovations

This book is a series of vignettes about changes to Australian institutions, organisations and systems that have significantly improved economic and social well-being for Australians. Economic system innovations have had a profound impact on our lives, from the invention of banking in the middle ages to the organisations established by the United Nations post-WWII. However, their intangible nature means that few people identify these changes alongside physical inventions.

Although invention is normally an incremental process, with copying and adaption being the norm, the authors focus on reforms that were principally new to the world at the time of implementation. The book is not about the reforms and how well they worked, per se, rather about the people and the political struggle to get them adopted. The authors have chosen to focus on the stories where Australia has either taken a global leadership role or made a considerable advance in a particular new institution. What these stories show is that leadership in institutional innovation can come from many quarters: academia, the community, politics and the bureaucracy. Often the most successful teams combine people from all quarters albeit with support from the fourth estate. The work shows how many reforms began with modest beginnings, often an ordinary person with a vision, and how it takes several attempts to get change accepted.

This key volume can be used to teach students of economics, political economy and politics. It illustrates the type of networks, actions and advocacy that is needed to get reform started and implemented and is written in a style to engage policy and think-tank audiences.

Beth Webster is Director of the Centre for Transformative Innovation at Swinburne University of Technology and Pro Vice Chancellor. She has a long abiding interest in economic research and the political economy of policy and has worked for several government departments and three public research institutes at Monash, Melbourne and Swinburne Universities.

Bill Scales has held governance, advisory and executive positions in business, industry, government and the not-for-profit sectors. These include manufacturing, telecommunications, the government sector, aged care, economic infrastructure and education sectors. He has been Chair or Panel Member on 13 major national and Australian state government inquiries and reviews across the economy.

Routledge Focus on Economics and Finance

The fields of economics are constantly expanding and evolving. This growth presents challenges for readers trying to keep up with the latest important insights. Routledge Focus on Economics and Finance presents short books on the latest big topics, linking in with the most cutting-edge economics research.

Individually, each title in the series provides coverage of a key academic topic, whilst collectively the series forms a comprehensive collection across the whole spectrum of economics.

Economics, Education and Youth Entrepreneurship
International Perspectives
Marian Noga and Andrzej Brzeziński

Markets vs Public Health Systems
Perspectives from the Austrian School of Economics
Łukasz Jasiński

Public Policy and the Impact of COVID-19 in Europe
Economic, Political and Social Dimensions
Magdalena Tomala, Maryana Prokop and Aleksandra Kordonska

Economic Innovations
Creating New Instruments to Improve Economic Life
Beth Webster and Bill Scales

Well-being and Growth in Advanced Economies
The Need to Prioritise Human Development
Maurizio Pugno

For more information about this series, please visit: www.routledge.com/ Routledge-Focus-on-Economics-and-Finance/book-series/RFEF

Economic Innovations
Creating New Instruments to Improve Economic Life

Beth Webster and Bill Scales

Routledge
Taylor & Francis Group

LONDON AND NEW YORK

First published 2023
by Routledge
4 Park Square, Milton Park, Abingdon, Oxon OX14 4RN

and by Routledge
605 Third Avenue, New York, NY 10158

Routledge is an imprint of the Taylor & Francis Group, an informa business

British Library Cataloguing-in-Publication Data
A catalogue record for this book is available from the British Library

Library of Congress Cataloging-in-Publication Data
Names: Webster, Beth, author. | Scales, Bill, author.
Title: Economic innovations : creating new instruments to improve
    economic life/Beth Webster and Bill Scales.
Description: Milton Park, Abingdon, Oxon ; New York : Routledge,
    2023. | Series: Routledge focus on economics and finance | Includes
    bibliographical references and index.
Identifiers: LCCN 2022014940 (print) | LCCN 2022014941 (ebook) |
    ISBN 9781032155142 (hardback) | ISBN 9781032155159 (paperback) |
    ISBN 9781003244424 (ebook)
Subjects: LCSH: Economics – Australia. | Australia – Economic
    conditions.
Classification: LCC HB129.A2 W43 2023 (print) | LCC HB129.A2
    (ebook) | DDC 330.994 – dc23/eng/20220404
LC record available at https://lccn.loc.gov/2022014940
LC ebook record available at https://lccn.loc.gov/2022014941

ISBN: 978-1-032-15514-2 (hbk)
ISBN: 978-1-032-15515-9 (pbk)
ISBN: 978-1-003-24442-4 (ebk)

DOI: 10.4324/9781003244424

Contents

About the authors

Beth Webster
Professor Beth Webster is Director of the Centre for Transformative Innovation at Swinburne University of Technology and Pro Vice Chancellor (Research Translation). She has a PhD (Cambridge), M Economics (Monash) and B Ec (hons) (Monash).

Her research interests cover several areas of applied economics including innovation; intangible capital; intellectual property; firm performance and public policy for the translation of science.

Under the name Elizabeth Webster she has authored over 100 articles on the economics of innovation and firm performance and has been published in *RAND Journal of Economics*, *Review of Economics and Statistics*, *Oxford Economic Papers, Journal of Law & Economics* and *Journal of International Economics*. She has been appointed to a number of committees including the Lomax-Smith Base Funding Review; the Bracks' Review of the Automotive Committee; CEDA Advisory Council; State Service Commission, the Advisory Council for Intellectual Property; European Policy for Intellectual Property Association; and Asia Pacific Innovation Network. She is a fellow of the Academy of Social Sciences Australia.

Bill Scales
Bill Scales has held governance, advisory and executive positions in business, industry, government and the not-for-profit sectors. His executive career has spanned manufacturing, telecommunications and the government sector including Group Managing Director, Telstra Corporation; Secretary, the Department of Premier and Cabinet in Victoria; Chairman and Chief Executive Officer, Industry Commission; Chairman and Chief Executive Officer, the Automotive Industry Authority among others.

Throughout his career Bill has also been Chair or Board Member of organisations within Australia's aged care, telecommunications, economic infrastructure and education sectors and Chair or Panel Member on 13 major national and Australian state government inquiries and reviews across the education, energy, industry, telecommunications and government sectors.

He is a qualified fitter and machinist, holds a Bachelor of Economics degree from Monash University and has completed the Harvard Business School's Advanced Management Program. He is an Officer of the Order of Australia; was awarded the Centenary Medal for outstanding service to business and commerce and has been awarded Honorary Doctorates from Swinburne University of Technology and Monash University. He is a national fellow of the Institute of Public Administration Australia, a life fellow of the Australian Institute of Company Directors and a senior fellow of the Economic Society of Australia.

Acknowledgements

We are deeply grateful to all the people, acknowledged in the footnote of each chapter for reading and correcting our first feeble drafts and for the oral histories from key people who were involved in the implementing of these marvellous innovations. It goes without saying that all errors remain ours alone and we apologise in advance if we have not named important contributors to the reforms. Hopefully, if we bring out a second edition, these omissions will be corrected.

Although we both contributed to the composition and writing of all chapters, one of us took primary responsibility for the first draft of each chapter, viz:

Bill Scales: A national system of industrial relations; The electoral system: the other invisible hand; Making a Federation work – the Grants Commission; Independent policy advice – the Productivity Commission; Comprehensive retirement income; Privatisating state enterprises; Managing a river basin – best practice or work-in-progress?; Australia's national electricity market – the NEM; Conclusion.

Beth Webster: Introduction; Pensions and benefits – earned or entitled?; Co-innovation in agriculture – the RDCs; Opening for business – dismantling import restrictions; Medicines for all – the PBS; Recognising poverty – the poverty line; Going metric; Universal health insurance – Medibank; Collecting financial support for children; Income-contingent student loans – HECS; A dispersed labour exchange – the Job Network; A national safety net for people with disabilities – the NDIS; A comprehensive business panel dataset – BLADE; and Evidence to understand household behaviours – HILDA.

1 Introduction

We all love the invention that gives us a new toy – a smart phone, an exciting car, a new game or fancy camera. But changes to economic institutions – contextual systems, rules, practices, rights and obligations – are less glamorous and, for most part, fly under the radar.

Yet these same institutions have delivered some of the largest improvements in the well-being of Australians over the last century. It's difficult to imagine Australia without Medicare, a social security system or a student loan system. Like the invention of goods, these 'overnight' successful changes in the social and economic infrastructure of Australia conceal many decades of agitating, fighting vested interests and staring down passive resistance. However, without the dedicated and singular pursuit by teams collaborating over a common vision, Australia might be still living with many of the social and economic structures of the 19th century with low farming and manufacturing productivity, an incomplete education and healthcare system and an idiosyncratic imperial measuring scheme.

This series of vignettes of Australian economic and public policy innovations is not about the reforms and how well they worked, but about the people and the political struggle to get the reforms adopted. The aim is to give the reader guidance on what they should do to implement their vision for the next generation of economic and public policy innovations. Our narratives do not aim to be a complete story of Australia's main reforms, or, of all the people who were involved in them. The stories we have highlighted are those where Australia has either taken a global leadership role or made a considerable advance on global practice.

Three key themes emerge from these examples. The first theme consists of the pre-conditions that led to the change being proposed. This includes the presence of a burning platform, the arrival of new technological opportunities and the social acceptance of an intellectual school of thought or idea. Hanging over the issues covered in this first theme lie the special challenges of Australia's geography.

DOI: 10.4324/9781003244424-1

The second theme involves examining common processes that are often necessary but not sufficient to get reforms implemented. Foremost is the necessity of establishing an alliance with a senior politician to champion the innovative idea and open doors for its implementation. But in addition, these examples demonstrate that for the successful implementation of economic and public policy innovation, there often needs to be strategies for mitigating opponents. New ideas need to be socialised within the relevant communities and this second theme examines how this has been done through widespread consultation with the effected groups, a judicious alignment with media and the use of scientific and economic evidence.

The third theme examines how, for some cases of economic and public policy innovation, institutional compromises need to be made to get final acceptance by pivotal parties. This may involve the creation of an independent ruling body or transitional arrangements for those negatively impacted.

Pre-conditions

Nothing focusses the mind on economic and public policy innovation more than a burning platform such as war or famine. Although Australia has avoided the scourge of famine, and war has not been fought on Australian soil, like many other nations it was impacted by two debilitating 20th century world wars. But in the second half of the 20th century, Australia was affected by a slow and an almost unrecognised loss of competitiveness. This and other threats have galvanised the minds, especially the minds of our politicians. The creation of the industrial relations system has been said to have been born from the bitter industrial disputes following the 1890s depression. This depression, and the poverty it created among older people, was also the drive to introduce a publicly funded 'universal' age pension. The student loan scheme, affectionately dubbed HECS, was a response to strong demand for higher education by the post-World War II 'baby-boomers', and its implications for government budgets. The urgency of reforms to the Murray-Darling basin water system was piqued by the devastating Millennium drought.

Australian was not immune from the arrival of new technologies that changed the cost-benefit calculations of many existing activities and 'suddenly' opened untapped opportunities. The advance of scientific medical knowledge and processes in the early 20th century made modern healthcare more reliable and efficacious. These developments led directly to expectations that medical care and pharmaceuticals should be accessible to all Australians and these expectations were ultimately realised via the introduction of Australia's Medibank and Pharmaceutical Benefits Scheme. Over the latter part of the 20th century, the pervasiveness of digital technologies gradually changed the configuration of value chains. Digital technologies made it possible to separate parts of the energy value chain – generation, transmission, wholesaleing and retailing – and effectively eroded natural monopolies, which in Australia's case were public natural monopolies. Once the grounds for public monopolies disappeared, Australia decided that there was no reason to limit entry of private sector competitors into this important market. Similarly, digital technologies have permitted the separation of funding, provision and payment in many human services. Australia was a leader in seizing the opportunity to make public employment services more fit-for-purpose.

Less obvious to householders has been the growth of more accurate data-bases which injected greater precision and more nuance into policy analysis. Better analysis leads directly to more efficient and effective business and social service policies. The Australian business and household longitudinal databases are only known to technical analysts, but their creation would not have been possible prior to the pervasive use of digital technologies. The same is true for our student loan scheme. Without the ability to eco-nomically and accurately link records between the education and taxation systems, the scheme would not have been practical.

Few of our innovations would have carried the day without intellectual antecedents from overseas. Australia's voting system, industrial relations structure and the universal age pension scheme can be directly traced to the historical school of social liberalism in Great Britain from the 18th and 19th centuries, and some argue that Australia's approach to industrial relations has its origins in progressive Catholic thought. The drive to reduce tariffs owns much to Ricardo's theory of trade which underpinned the 1830s corn-law debates in Great Britain. These ideas were carried with force to Austra-lia where there has been a tradition of producing internationally acclaimed trade economists. The idea of measuring poverty, and the subsequent vision for a guaranteed minimum income for children, can be traced to early 20th century survey work in Wales. The income contingent student loan scheme was the brain-child of two American economists and the idea for a disabil-ity insurance scheme came from a New Zealand judge. Privatisation was an old idea but came back into fashion, first in the United Kingdom, in the mid-20th century. And finally, both of our panel datasets, household and business, were created after seeing prototypes from the USA from the 1960s and 1980s respectively.

Finally, the special geography and population of Australia has compelled it to innovate, or innovate in different ways, from the rest of the world. This is apparent with the formation of the rural R&D corporations. Agriculture has always been a major Australian export sector, but exports can only be sustained by continually moving with the frontier of efficiency. This was simply not going to happen if we relied on sole innovators working away on remote farms. Collective action was required. Less apparent but not necessarily less needed was the role of national governments in the social security and industrial relations systems. When parties are dispersed and separate it is much harder for market mechanisms and collective agencies to form naturally.

Processes

To some extent ideas are cheap. They are the fun part of reform. By contrast, the heavy slog of realising cogent ideas, that is, ideas that are clear, logical and convincing can consume lives and test the dedication of even extraordinary people.

Most major reforms need the assent of a nation's Parliament and therefore the active work, if not the backing, of a champion politician. The quest to be the first jurisdiction to introduce a universal age pension was viewed as a race between the parliaments of New Zealand, New South Wales and Victoria, with the Victorian Premier being most piqued for being last by a few months. In Australia, reforms such as the development of the rural R&D bodies, the establishment of an economic reform commission, superannuation, the Pharmaceutical Benefits Scheme and the Murray-Darling water management plans were largely bipartisan, albeit, often with the opposition party stymying the plans of the government-of-the-day in order to introduce their own similar plan when in office.

Other Australian reforms, such as the introduction of universal healthcare, disability insurance and the use of the tax office to collect child support were hard fought battles. It took senior Australian Labor Government ministers the larger part of their time in office to win people over. In these cases, it needed the Prime Minister to step in to tell recalcitrant bureaucrats to just 'do it'. Interestingly, the reforms around tariffs and student loans were not traditional Labor party issues but were taken up by Labor politicians who realised that some of the Labor mantras were undermining not only Australia's competitiveness, but also their own goals of social and economic justice. Although the conservative side of politics tended to stick to their traditional market-orientated reforms, such as privatisation, their support for the rural R&D units was a page out of the socialist book.

Few reforms sail through without the need to mitigate opponents and raise awareness among potential beneficiaries. In Australia the medical establishment has sometimes been the most trenchant opponent of anything that brushes against their turf. Universal health care was on the radar soon after World War II but was fiercely opposed at every turn by the medical and health insurance associations. These opponents fought at both the emotional and political level and managed to forestall a national health insurance scheme by three decades. This is now seen as ironic given that few doctors now opt to work outside the scheme. Australian manufacturers had clear incentives to oppose Australia's tariff reduction program in the 1980s and 1990s and much work needed to be done by politicians, backed by evidence from economists in academia and the public service, to disarm them. Australian university students and others within the tertiary education sector were outraged by the prospect of student fees – little would convince them of the economic arguments – and the government and its advisors just forced these reforms through. In both these cases, it took a lot of work by Labor Government politicians to neutralise the opposition to these reforms from the Labor Party rank and file. The unions and philanthropic sector may have had qualms about outsourcing employment services, but these melted when they realised that it offered a business opportunity for themselves and a more effective means of getting the unemployed into work.

Many innovations were opposed or passively resisted by government departments in parts of the public service. The Federal minister for agriculture had to neutralise the views of Treasury in relation the introduction of Rural R&D units because it did not favour this level of intervention in the market; the household longitudinal database was outsourced to a university as its department of social security creators did not believe the statistics bureau would deliver a research-ready database; the department of social security was openly hostile to new ways of collecting child support; the tax office was antagonistic to assisting both the child support unit to collect child support from the responsible parent and the student loans unit to collect student HECS fees; State bureaucrats needed to be made comfortable about being overtaken by a national disability scheme; the attorney generals department resisted the loss of control over child support arrangements; and successive generations of health departments simply believed that reforms to the health care system were not possible.

Socialising ideas, so that the relevant population is not affronted by economic and social change and alerting the community to the hidden beneficiaries of existing poor policy has been undertaken by most reformers. For many policy innovations this was done by actively meeting with people. In the 1960s when Australia adopted the metric system of measurement, the metrification implementation agencies held many town hall meetings with local communities, met with all industry bodies and employed an army of foot soldiers to speak directly to traders and manufacturers about how to make the change. The reforms in the Murray-Darling river basin were also played out through countless, often acrimonious, town hall meetings; and a wide range of people from civil society contributed to the debate about an aged pension and the national disability insurance scheme. Less visible but more focussed meetings and conferences were held over the benefits of reducing tariffs. Even more technical meetings took place among the economics cognoscenti on the need for a business longitudinal database.

The media was often brought in as an ally to profile the need for economic and social change. This was most apparent in the tariff debates – the business media were especially pro-tariff reduction. The media was a critical contributor in broadcasting information about the magnitude of poverty in Australia in the 1960s and its effects, as it still does today. Both the proponents of universal health care and conversion to the metric system used the media widely to explain to the population what was going to happen. Disability reformers briefed sympathetic journalists and used social media to corral their dispersed coalition of supporters in support of a national disability scheme for Australia. As we would expect, the media was also used by the opponents of change. The medical establishment was especially canny in presenting a case that government interference in the provision of health care would amount to socialism within Australia's medical system and an intrusion into the sanctified relationship between doctors and their patients.

Over and above these activities, formal consultations with stakeholders were also used by policy innovators to qualify and nuance the nature of their proposed innovation. This was especially true for the establishment of the Grants Commission, the mode of conversion to metric measurement by each industry, and users' requirements with respect to the household and business longitudinal databases.

Allied with this was the use by policy innovators of purpose-built scientific and economic evidence. Scientific evidence was used successfully to get interested parties to also focus on long-term environmental issues rather than just the immediate use of water for agriculture. Economic analysis is almost always used to set out clearly the trade-offs involved in not making a change. The concept of opportunity cost is basic bread and butter to all economists but is often a strange and novel concept to others. Nowhere was this most apparent than in the work done by academics and the Productivity Commission (and its predecessors) over planned reductions to import restrictions. It took many reports and inquiries for the export sector and the consuming household sector to appreciate the personal cost to them of import tariffs. Similar calculations were made to illustrate the economic inefficiency associated with public business monopolies. Economic evidence was used to show people the ongoing costs savings associated with conversion to metric measurement, the benefits to both children and the department of finance of getting better compliance with child support orders and to disabled people for better targeted assistance. Finally, evidence was used by Ronald Henderson to shame the prime minister of the day into taking poverty seriously.

Compromising for an outcome

Achieving the level of consensus needed for change can mean introducing independent or improved governance mechanisms. In the case of the Grants Commission, the electoral commission, the rural R&D units, the Pharmaceutical Benefits Scheme, the Productivity Commission and the household longitudinal database, placing responsibility for oversight or operation in a new or independent body was not only politic but the only way to get sceptical stakeholders to acquiesce. Other innovations which operated within existing structures, such as child support collection, the business longitudinal database, and the student loans unit, had new rules established to ensure probity and compliance with the law.

Transitional measures have been essential for innovations that are predicted to lead to major economic or social disruptions. Chief among these are the tariff reforms. Max Corden, an eminent Australian economist, very explicitly advocated for a gradual simplification and then reduction of import barriers, and, in relation to tariff reforms directed at the Australian auto industry, the Button Car Plan, and later plans from the Bracks and Green Reviews of the Australian auto industry, had programs to help affected businesses refocus their markets, or close, in an orderly manner. The team leading the conversion to metric measurement ensured that each industry chartered its own transition, so they felt empowered and part of the process. Workers and employers were given trade-offs as part of a social compact that included compulsory superannuation. Fees for higher education courses were introduced at a very modest level and the new child support package was split into easy and hard parts in order to make the change more gradual.

To conclude

What these stories about Australian economic and social reform show is that leadership in institutional innovation can come from many quarters: academia, the community, politics and the bureaucracy. Often the most successful teams combine people from all quarters albeit with support from the fourth estate. Few reforms sail through without resistance and many ideas take three, four or more attempts to socialise among key decision-making groups. However, these stories show that economic and social reforms matter to the welfare of Australians, and that Australia is capable of introducing difficult reforms, even the face of what sometimes seems like overwhelming resistance.

2 Establishing national foundations

A national system of industrial relations

From the very beginning of the Commonwealth of Australia, Australia has had a unique system for the settling of industrial disputes and for the general setting of what was described early in Australia's history as a basic or minimum wage. After New Zealand, Australia established one of the first *national* minimum wages in the world. The basic principles for setting Australia's wages, conditions and industrial disputation for over 60 years was determined primarily by the principles set down in what has become known as the 'Harvester' Judgement.

A curious element of Australia's early wage and industrial disputes settling procedures is that the Harvester Judgement was only tangentially related to the settling of wages or industrial disputes. The Harvester Judgement actually laid down the rules for charging an excise tariff, designed as part of Australia's early inclination for government intervention and protection of industry. Australia has a long history of debate and argument about if, and how to best regulate relations between workers and their employers. Some of these debates and arguments have been long and bloody. These debates have not been contained to just the relationship between employers and their workers but have also been central in debates about Australia's economic development.

In the context of Australia's industrial relations framework, the Harvester Judgement of 1907 is important for several reasons. Although it was not a ruling to resolve an industrial dispute that cut across state borders, it was to become a benchmark for the setting of minimum wages for the next 60 years and was inextricably linked to the level of tariff protection provided to several Australian industries, particularly those in the manufacturing sector.

DOI: 10.4324/9781003244424-2

This issue is complicated and needs a bit of 'unpacking'

To look sensibly at the Harvester Decision and its long-term implications for Australia and Australia's unique industrial relations system, we need to look at an important part of Australia's history before and leading up to the establishment of the Commonwealth of Australia in 1901. Australia's very early approach to settling industrial disputes could be best described as a series of experiments. In its early days, the colony of New South Wales had rudimentary rules regarding the employment of convicts. These rudimentary rules were replaced in 1828 by the New South Wales Masters and Servants Act, which established rules for disciplining employees. Once some form of democratic government was established within the Australian colonies, each colony developed some form of industrial regulation more acceptable to their constituents.

In 1873, Victoria gave some protection to workers through its Shops and Factories Act, and in 1881 New South Wales passed the Trade Union Act which gave workers rights to form trade unions. Other colonies soon followed with their own versions of basic industrial laws. However, these systems varied from Victoria, where separate wages boards were established to hear and determine matters from certain industries, to New South Wales where parties tended to meet to sort out their issues under the watchful eye of an independent chair. Importantly, at the time, whereas nations such as the United States of America, Britain, Canada and other industrialised nations learned from these Australian experiments, they maintained their systems of collective bargaining, wherein wages and conditions were primarily determined by agreement between employers and their employees.

In the 1890s, notwithstanding these early attempts by the Australian colonies to regulate wages and conditions and avoid industrial conflicts, Australia was for the very first time confronted with a number of debilitating industrial disputes that have been described by historians as 'The Great Strikes'. These industrial disputes included the 1890 maritime strike, the 1891 and 1894 shearer's strikes and the strike in 1892 that significantly affected the operations of mining at Broken Hill. A number of these strikes were long, violent, bloody and bitter (Fair Work Australia 2011, p. 12). These strikes caused significant unease across the colonies and led to the setting up of a Royal Commission in New South Wales on the cause of the strikes. The question of how to address industrial disputes was a sub-set of the larger issue of whether the yet-to-be determined constitution for Australia should allow the Commonwealth Government to enter into labour issues.

After a tense and sometimes bitter debate, and through the significant persuasive power of Henry Bourne Higgins, and Charles Kingston, the Colonial Premier of South Australia, by a vote of 22 to 19, the Constitutional Convention eventually voted that section 51(35) of the Australian Constitution should provide the yet to be established Commonwealth Parliament with the right to legislate with respect to '*conciliation and arbitration for the prevention and settlement of industrial disputes extending beyond the limits of one state*' (Fair Work Australia 2011, p. 12).

The direct effect of these long and bitter industrial disputes of the late 1800s was that one of the very first matters addressed by the fledgling Commonwealth of Australia in 1901 was to consider whether the new Parliament should legislate a process for addressing industrial matters in the future, and whether the Commonwealth should allocate to itself a means of doing so. Justice Michael Kirby has argued that it's an 'over-simplification' to suggest that the Commonwealth's eventual role in this area of human activity was what he describes as 'simply' a result of the bitter disputes of the 1890s; however, they were clearly a contributor (Kirby 2004, p. 7).

This debate continued for many years after the establishment of the Commonwealth, within and without the new parliament. The level of disagreement and confusion about the role that this new Commonwealth should play in this important area cannot be underestimated. The Conciliation and Arbitration Act began its passage through the Parliament in May 1901 and was not passed by the Parliament until 1904. During debates on the legislation to establish a role for the Commonwealth in this area, there were four changes of government and four changes of Prime Ministers – Barton, Deakin, Watson and Reid. Bitter divisions about the Commonwealth's role in setting wages and conditions for workers and settling certain industrial disputes brought about three of these changes of Government and Prime Ministers (Kirby 2004, p. 13).

In 1904, and after protracted, difficult and often confusing debate in the new Australian Parliament, the Commonwealth Conciliation and Arbitration Act was born to address industrial disputes that extended beyond state borders. When the Commonwealth Government decided to establish a direct role in resolving certain industrial disputes, Australia became the only nation at that time to adopt compulsory conciliation and arbitration for resolving national disputes between employees and their workers, that is, disputes that cut across sub-national borders. Although each individual state government maintained their own industrial systems and regulations, they were eventually to become subservient to the key elements of the Commonwealth's system.

The Commonwealth Conciliation and Arbitration Act also brought with it a new institution, the Commonwealth Court of Conciliation and Arbitration.

Not surprisingly, once the legislation was passed and the Conciliation and Arbitration Court was established, the very first decisions of this brand-new institution covered two of those industries involved in the Great Strikes of the 1890s, the maritime and the shearing industries.

There was one other development that cemented the unique, and to some extent curious nature of Australia's system of conciliation and arbitration, particularly in relation to the setting of wages. This was the link in 1906 between the imposition by the Commonwealth of an excise tariff on some goods manufactured in Australia, including agricultural implements, and the wages paid to their workers. Although the imposition of this excise tariff was very soon after its implementation to be found constitutionally invalid, this little known element of Australia's wage fixing system is important because of its long-term implications on Australia's industrial relations and economic environment.

This excise tariff was part of what was described at the time as the New Protection. This New Protection had two elements. The first was the imposition of an import tariff on goods coming into Australia. The second element of this policy was the imposition of an excise tariff on goods produced in Australia. If the producers of domestically produced goods did not pay their workers what was described in the legislation as a 'fair and reasonable wage' then an excise tax would be imposed. The customs tariff was set for a stripper harvester at 12 pounds, and the excise tariff on an Australian Harvester was set at 6 pounds – both significant amounts of money in the early 1900s.

However, and here it starts to get a bit complicated. If a manufacturer of agricultural implements could prove that it was paying 'fair and reasonable wages', then it could seek the removal of the imposition of any excise tariff on its products manufactured in Australia, giving it a competitive advantage in both the Australian and in export markets. It is very important to emphasise that this excise tariff was separate, and very different from the import tariffs that had been an important part of the revenue-raising armoury of the early colonies and was ceded by the colonies to the Commonwealth at the time of federation.

Clearly, it was in the interests of manufacturers upon which this excise tariff was imposed, to seek it removed, based on their assertion that they were paying fair and reasonable wages. But this created the first complication. What exactly is 'fair and reasonable' wages?

Unsurprisingly, almost immediately after its imposition, 112 local producers of agricultural equipment applied to the newly established Conciliation and Arbitration Court to have this considerable impost removed by attempting to prove that they were in fact paying fair and reasonable wages to their workers. Amongst these early applicants was HV McKay, one of the largest manufacturers of combine harvesters and other agricultural machinery upon which this excise duty was applied.

Consideration of this matter, which was important, not only for the Harvester Company, but also for many other Australian manufacturers was undertaken by the second President of the Conciliation and Arbitration Court, the Honourable Henry Bournes Higgins. Higgins picked the case put forward by HV McKay, the owner of the Harvester Company, located in Sunshine, an industrial suburb of Melbourne, as a sample case because he expected that this case would be hotly contested.

Higgins was no newcomer to the debates across Australia about the role of the new Parliament and the courts in relation to the settling of disputes between organisations and their workers, especially in relation to those organisations that transcended State borders. He had been heavily involved in the debates on this issue in the lead up to the establishment of the Commonwealth of Australia and was one of Victoria's 10 delegates to the Convention of 1897–1899 that eventually constructed the Commonwealth Constitution. After a somewhat mixed history in State politics in Victoria, Higgins became a member of the newly formed Australian Parliament, representing the constituency of North Melbourne. Higgins was a strong advocate for the new Commonwealth playing a role in settling industrial disputes.

In 1906, Higgins became a justice of the High Court of Australia, where he remained until his death in 1929. Concurrent with his role on the High Court, Higgins served as President of the Conciliation and Arbitration Court (Rickard 2020). In hearing the case put forward by HV McKay for the removal of the excise tariff, Justice Higgins decided that a fair and reasonable wage should be set at 7 shillings a day for an unskilled labourer. Justice Higgins determined that 7 shillings a day was a wage sufficient to allow an unskilled labourer to support himself, a wife and three children.

Notwithstanding that in handing down this decision in 1907 Higgins had no actual evidence of a labourer's budget, and based his decision on the scant evidence he had before him of the household budgets of just 11 tradesmen from seven different trades, and only seven general categories of expenditures, Rent: Food: Fuel and light: Boots/clothes: Fares: Insurance: and Other (Fair Work Australia 2011, pp. 60–61). This decision of Justice Higgins reverberated across Australia's industrial landscape for over 60 years and became the cornerstone for the setting of Australia's minimum wage.

Ironically, very soon after its imposition on manufacturers, the excise duty imposed by the Commonwealth was found to be invalid by the High Court of Australia, with Higgins dissenting. However, the concepts set by Higgins as to what constituted a fair wage remained. The Harvester Judgement also rejected the notion that minimum wages should be set by reference to an employer's ability to pay (Ex Parte, HV McKay 1907; Commonwealth Arbitration Report Volume 2, 1907, pp. 1–2, p. 5).

The role of the Harvester Judgement in Australia's political and industrial history is important and curious. Important because in terms of global industrial relations systems, the Harvester Judgement set the preconditions for establishing a highly centralised and proscriptive system for the setting of national wages and settling of industrial disputes. Curious because whereas the Harvester Judgement was central in Australia's system of settling industrial disputes, the Harvester Case of 1907 was not actually a case about settling an industrial dispute. It was a case about determining whether an excise tariff, a local production tax if you like, should be applied to the production of certain agricultural products. It is curious because when determining what constituted a fair and reasonable wage, Higgins had little evidence to support the Court's judgement and Higgins's decision in this case seemed to be decided on his own personal beliefs.

'I cannot think that an employer and a workman contract on an equal footing, or make a "fair" agreement to wages, when the workman submits to work for a low wage to avoid starvation or pauperism (or something like it) for himself and his family; or that the agreement is "reasonable" if it does not carry a wage sufficient to ensure the workman food, shelter, clothing, frugal comfort, provision for evil days, (etc.) as well as award for special skill of an artisan if he is one' (Ex Parte, HV McKay 1907, Commonwealth Arbitration Report Volume 2 1907, p. 4).

Curious also because the decision of the Court to apply a seven shillings a day standard for a labourer would be required to be paid to a labourer, even if he was not married, and had no children to support.

If the decision by Higgins was not based on the facts of the case, how did Higgins's personal views come about? It has been speculated that the decision of Justice Higgins, a northern Irish protestant, was influenced by the social teachings of the Catholic Church, and in particular of the encyclical of Pope Leo the XIII Rerum Novarum, that among other matters, covered what constitutes fair wages. Both Justice Michael Kirby and Bob Hawke, Australia's 23rd, and longest serving Labour Prime Minister have argued that Higgins was influenced by his own religious upbringing and that he embraced ideas in Rerum Novarum (Kirby 2004, p. 5; Hawke 2010, pp. 2–3). However, Fr. Frank Brennan, a Jesuit priest, lawyer and theologian is more sceptical. '*I have my doubts that Higgins would have been directly influenced all that much by Pope Leo's writing in Rerum Novarum except in so far as the papal utterances reflected the thinking of many fairminded people at the time, regardless of their political affiliations at the time*' (Brennan 2017).

The Harvester Judgement is also fascinating because the first industrial dispute to use the principles set down in the Harvester Judgement was the case in 1907 of 'The Marine Cooks, Bakers, and Butchers' Association of Australia versus The Commonwealth Steam Ship Owners Association (also presided over by Justice H V Higgins). It is helpful here to quote Higgins from his judgement from the transcript of the judgement of this case to show how he was able to use the concepts from the decision he made in the Harvester Case to set the principles he would apply in industrial disputation cases involving the direct setting of wages.

'No doubt the issue is not the same as the Harvester Case, – and yet the same considerations are necessary. I must settle the dispute on terms which seem to me just, on terms which I deem to be fair and reasonable between the parties'. – 'and I cannot conceive any term to be fair and reasonable which does not at the very least allow a man to live from his labour, to live as a human being in a civilized community' ('The Marine Cooks, Bakers, and Butchers' Association of Australia v The Commonwealth Steam Ship Owners Association, 1907/08 2 CAR 55: p. 60, p. 61).

The establishment of comprehensive arrangements for considering and determining industrial relations matters was uniquely Australian. In addition, the decision in 1907 by Australia's newly established Conciliation and Arbitration Court to determine that a fair and reasonable wage for a labourer was based on the ability of an unskilled labourer to support a wife and three children, and to feed, house and clothe them just might also fit the definition of being unique (Fair Work Australia 2011, p. 65).

Higgins's decisions, whatever his motivations, both in the Harvester Judgement, to determine whether a company was paying fair and reasonable wages for the purpose of relief from an excise tariff, and in the Marine Cooks, Bakers and Butchers Association case, would reverberate across Australia for over 60 years. These two cases would establish the principles for Australia's basic wage. Whether Australia benefited in the long run from these two judgements by Higgins in the early 1900s is still a matter of debate. But what is not debatable is that the decision by the Australian Commonwealth's early parliaments set the template for implementation of Australia's unique approach to industrial relations and that the Higgins decisions irreversibly determined the character of that approach.

Pensions and benefits – earned or entitled?[1]

Societies have always had supporting mechanisms for those unable to provide for themselves. At its most basic, this role fell to the family or local charities. Since 1536, the English Poor Law allowed local parishes to levy rates on landowners to run poor houses and offer relief payments (Garton 2008;

Kunze 1971). In Australia, in the period immediately after white settlement, distance and a primitive social infrastructure made the development of a coherent social support system for those unable to provide for themselves largely impractical. Consequently, government monies were used to supplement local charities which decided who did, and did not, get relief (Garton 2008). These arrangements became strained in Australia during the 1890s economic depression when riots and severe economic distress led Australian colonial governments to increase public relief work and pay a dole. These measures did not however solve the problem of overcrowding and the imprisonment of destitute elderly people (Dixon 1983).

The 1890s depression in Australia laid bare the gaps and cracks in Australia's social security system, foremost of which was the lack of sustenance for old people. According to Dixon (1983) in-kind transfers were considered an acceptable solution by the smaller Australian colonial States, but leaders in NSW, Victoria and those in New Zealand, which had a historically close association with Australia, thought that this did not tackle the root cause of destitution. They agreed that something systematic needed to be done. The question was what.

Overseas, Bismarck had led the way in the 1880s by introducing compulsory contributory sickness and accident insurance for German workers and an old age pension program funded by contributions from employers, workers and government (Hennock 2003). His policies sprang from the historical school of economics and social liberalism thought that emanated from the United Kingdom and the United States. The insurance part was not new as modern life insurance had existed since the 1750s. What was new was the compulsion and the requirement for employers to contribute (Plummer 1927).

In Australia, many parties weighed into the 1890s debate about the adequacy and the future structure of Australia's social security system – ministers of religion, judges, the benevolent societies, philanthropists, bureaucrats, trade unions, physicians and of course parliamentarians (Encel 1996). At stake were two main decisions. First, whether any future scheme was to operate like a personal insurance scheme whereby workers paid-as-they-went and were then supported pro rata when needed. This is called a contributory scheme. The alternative was to fund support from general government revenues whereby benefits are not actuarially derived from individual contributions. Second, was who should be covered – both men and women? All ages? All races? Even the 'undeserving'?

In 1896, a NSW Select Committee, led by John Cash Neild and Edward O'Sullivan, was appointed to investigate the matter. A contributory scheme was rejected early on (Kewley 1973 as cited in Sawer 2012). It would not be administratively feasible and would not solve the immediate problem of poverty among the old and infirm, women (married or widowed) and the sick (Dixon 1983). Furthermore, the Committee argued that the working classes would be unable to sustain contributions and it would not solve the evident poverty among the aged, especially women.

This debate about support for the needs of older people to be seen in the context of an 'unusual alignment of class and ideological forces . . . the labour movement, [and] the progressive character of colonial liberalism' (Murphy 2021, p. 1). According to Murphy (2008) and Dickey (1980), 19th-century Australian leaders were often students or followers of radical European thinkers on the ethical role of the state, the liberal doctrine of universal rights and the labour movement. People, not owners of land and machines, created wealth and therefore people had a right to a share of the nation's wealth.

However, there were nuances. Murphy has revealed that the debates in NSW and Victoria sprang from philosophically different premises. In NSW, arguments for pensions were associated with the rights of workers to a fair wage. In addition, reasonable minimum wages and old age pensions were the means to prevent the under-consumption which had plagued capitalism since its inception. Bernhard Ringrose Wise, the NSW attorney-general and student of the social reformer, Thomas Green, was involved in both the arbitration and old age pension acts (Sawer 2012). Sydney, in particular, was influenced by an organised labour movement and a progressive Catholic social thought stemming from the 1891 Papal encyclical Rerum Novarum (Murphy 2008). Across the ditch in New Zealand, similar discussions were being held and the New Zealand Liberal Government of John Ballance made New Zealand the first Australasian country to introduce progressive income and land tax in 1891–1892, and, a non-contributory age pension in 1989 (Sawer 2012).

By contrast, Murphy (2008, p. 38) describes the debate in Victoria as a '19th-century combination of sanctimonious nonconformity and censorious morality' with proposed differences for the 'deserving and less deserving'. The Protestant work ethic permeated the discussions as it was assumed that self-governing civilized individuals produced the most robust societies. As today, there were moral hazard concerns about the effect of certain safety nets on individuals' work ethic and thrift (Dixon 1983).

There was a contest between jurisdictions to be first with a non-contributory age pension scheme. New Zealand won by passing its legislation in October 1898, followed by NSW and then Victoria in 1900. The Victorian Premier, George Turner, was reportedly irritated for being last by a few months. All schemes had exclusions for Chinese and indigenous Australians, and all had a character test to exclude those who had not led a sober and reputable life.

At the heart of the drive for a non-contributory system was the ambition for a safety net available to all members of society. No longer would there be holes into which those who had not had the ability or opportunity to work might fall. Combined with a means test, the scheme was deemed affordable and reasonably progressive.

Institutions, their rules and societal expectations, are path dependent. The non-contributory nature of these first age pensions set the standard for the other States and the subsequent national age pension scheme which was introduced by the fledging Federal Government (in 1908). When the national child endowment, a widows' pension, wife and children's allowance and unemployment, sickness and special benefits were introduced by the Federal Government in the 1940s, they were also funded by general government revenue (ABS 1988; Herscovitch and Stanton 2008).

The contributory nature of Bismarck's pension scheme was subsequently copied by other continental European nations (except in Denmark) and remains the cornerstone of their social security system today. A lack of interest in contributory schemes in Australia can be attributed to established social norms. The Cook Government in 1913, the Bruce/Page Government in 1928 and the Lyons Government in 1938 all examined the virtues of a contributory scheme but did not implement them due to widespread opposition to such schemes (Daniels 2011).

The electoral system: the other invisible hand[2]

Voting systems are central to the acceptance of the legitimacy of that nation's political system. Given the importance of politicians and parliament in innovation and reform, the quality of the voting system is central for ensuring the health of the economy.

Australia's system of voting has from the beginning of Australia's formation been a critical element in the development of Australia as a robust and effective democracy. It is an unrecognised supporter of Australia's ability to meet its social, political and economic challenges. Importantly, Australia was an innovator and early adopter of a number of important electoral reforms. These consist of: compulsory voting; the early provision of voting rights to women; the use of preferential voting; a uniform national approach to the conduct of elections; voting on Saturdays; secret ballot; the conducting of elections by bureaucrats without any direct involvement by elected officials; and importantly, a transparent and independent approach to the establishment and redistribution of electoral boundaries (Brett 2019).

Mancur Olson captures the fundamental essence of the symbiotic relationship between economics and politics when he says that '[t]he economies move the polities and the polities govern the economies . . . theories . . . [in which] politics . . . is exogenous – are inherently limited and unbalanced' (Olson 2000, p. xxxvii). Olson expands on this concept by further arguing that in any discussion about economic and political development, in addition to Adam Smith's invisible hand of the market there needs to be a discussion about a second invisible hand: 'There can be no satisfactory theory of power, of government and politics, of the good and the harm done by governments to economies, that leave out the second invisible hand' (Olson, 2000, p. 13).

Consistent with Olson's perspective that economics and politics are inextricably intertwined, a trusted voting system must be part of that endogenous political invisable hand. A trustworthy and reliable voting system is one of the fundamental institutions of a healthy economic and political system. It stands along-side the rule of law as one of the foundation institutions of a just, sophisticated, civil and civic society that makes the very best use of society's resources.

Since Federation in 1901, Australian leaders have understood the importance of a trustworthy and reliable voting system in the development of the young democracy. According to Brett, the dominant view among Australians was that most people should vote, and elections should be orderly and run by government officials (Brett 2019, p. 2). Australia has not always been the first in terms of electoral reforms, but has always been at the forefront, especially in relation to voting rights and electoral administrative reform, with one important and serious exception. That exception was its ignorance for 80 years in relation to the voting rights of Australia's First Peoples, its indigenous Aboriginal people.

Most who are interested in the efficacy of electoral systems understand that electoral systems are most often determined by the history of a country, not necessarily by the logic inherent in the system itself. And, once established they are affected by the principles of path dependency, that is, once a particular path is well established, it is very difficult to divert from that path. Although Australia was not always world best-practice in electoral systems, it has cared deeply about its electoral system, has become aware over time of its inadequacies and has done something about them.

From Federation in 1901, Australia has quite explicitly created a system of representative government consisting of the (lower) House of Representatives and the (upper) Senate house. Notwithstanding early debates, the right to vote excluded some indigenous Australians, non-European migrants, and for a very short time, women from voting in national elections. However, the over-riding expectation was that the political system will adopt an expansive view of those qualified to vote in elections. This can be seen in the way that the Australian polity has continued to expand the right to vote and to protect those rights.

In 1924, when compulsory voting was introduced, Australia was one of the few nations in the world not only with compulsion but also with penalties, albeit token (Australian Electoral Commission 2019a, p. 1). The idea of compulsory voting is still an oddity internationally and seen by some nations as undermining the civil rights of an individual (International

Institute for Democracy and Electoral Assistance, 2021). However, for Australia, the idea of compulsory voting has a logic. It is anchored in the idea that all Australians are expected to participate in its polity. Making voting compulsory reduces the need for people to be coaxed, bribed if you like or encouraged by arguments that appealed to their base instincts or interests to attend the polls to vote. Brett documents how this argument dates back to the mid-19th century in Australia, and has its origins not only in the desire to encourage Australians to participate in the political processes through their right to vote, but also as a response to what many recent migrants from Great Britain saw as the deficiencies in the British system (Brett 2019, pp. 11–14, pp. 94–110).

The Australian Electoral Commission reported that 96.8% of eligible voters were enrolled to vote in the 2019 national election. Of these, 92%, or 15.08 million people voted, with 94.5% of votes in the House of Representatives and 96.2% of votes in the Senate being valid votes. These results show a high acceptance by Australians of compulsory voting and a strong willingness to actively participate in this basic element of the political process (Australian Electoral Commission 2019b). The Australian National University, which has conducted the Australian Election Study since 1987, found that in 2019 the top three issues on which electors cast their votes were the economy (24%), health (22%) and the environment (21%) (Cameron and McAllister 2019a, p. 7). This tendency towards voting on policy issues has been an increasing trend in Australian federal elections for over 20 years and gives force to the view that compulsory voting does not undermine Australians' willingness to inform themselves and participate in issues (Cameron and McAllister 2019b, p. 24).

From the very beginning of Australian Federation in 1901, the new Australian Parliament had a strong disposition for a broad definition of who would be eligible to vote in national elections. However, there were discriminatory carve outs. First Nation's people were excluded until the 1960s unless they were enrolled for State elections. Australia granted women the right to vote in 1902, one year after Federation, and behind New Zealand which granted women this right in 1893.

Another distinctive feature of Australia's system of voting is preferential voting. Prior to 1918, Australia operated under a 'first past the post' system of voting. Australia introduced preferential voting for the House of Representatives in 1918 and in 1948, an alternative form of preferential voting, called proportional representation for voting for the Senate. Although the use of preferential voting is not central to the application of Olson's concept of the second invisible hand, it is central to the way Australia sees itself. Preferential voting ensures the governments are generally supported by the largest number of its citizens as possible. It means if their first preference does not attract 50% of the votes, their vote may count towards a second option. Preferential voting provides the Australian people with more skin in the game when it comes to the selection of their parliamentary representatives than if they were choosing their representative through the 'first past the post' method.

The seriousness with which the fledging Commonwealth Government took to the fair and independent conduct of its national elections is demonstrated by the fact that one of the very first acts of the new Commonwealth Government was deciding on who can vote, and importantly, how voting was to be conducted. By early 1902, just one year after swearing in of the new Commonwealth Government of Australia, the prescribed methods of conducting national elections was passed. However just as importantly, six months earlier, in June of 1901, and even before the passing of the relevant legislation, electoral officials of the new Commonwealth Government and the States met to determine the principles upon which national elections would be conducted (Brett 2019, p. 73).

However, they didn't stop there. They went on to define in some detail the administrative system that would ensure that this was to come about, while ensuring that politicians would be removed from the process of conducting these elections. They agreed that there would be a Chief Electoral Officer for the Commonwealth; a Commonwealth electoral officer for each state and an electoral officer for each electoral division within each state. To ensure as much as possible the independence of these officials, they agreed that they would all be permanent, salaried public servants, independent of the political processes; their various duties would be clearly defined by law and their duties would be transparently detailed in printed instructions.

An other important element of Australia's attempt to construct a robust and trustworthy approach to electoral matters is the way by which the establishment and redistribution of electoral boundaries are determined. As is now well understood and acknowledged, confidence in electoral systems is quickly undermined, and with it, confidence in Olson's second invisible hand if an electoral system is subject to a 'gerrymander'. That is, the manipulation of electoral boundaries for unfair partisan political purposes.

The Australian Electoral Commission has a responsibility to independently assess the requirements for the redrawing of electoral boundaries for the House of Representatives. There is no requirement for the redefining of electoral boundaries for the Australian Senate. This is because the minimum number of members of the Senate are determined by the Australian Constitution, with each State having the same number of Senators, irrespective of the number of voters. In relation to the Australian Territories, the Northern Territory has one Senator, and the Australian Capital Territory two. In relation to the Australian House of Representatives it is the Australian Electoral Commission, not politicians or the National Parliament that determines the final structure of the electoral boundaries. The electoral boundaries for the

House of Representatives are regularly reviewed by the Australian Electoral Commission.

As discussed previously, one important exception to Australia's acknowledged enlightened approach to electoral matters is its approach until the 1980s to the provision of voting rights to its Aboriginal people. Australia's approach to the provision of voting rights to its Aboriginal people is hard to justify, even today. After Federation in 1901, some States provided some Aboriginals with voting rights in certain circumstances. All Australia's Aboriginal people were not provided with the right to vote until 1962, and all of Australia's Aboriginal people were not required to conform to the same voting requirements as all other Australians, including compulsory voting, until 1983 (Brett 2019, pp. 56–72). Today, Australia's system of voting does not differentiate between Australia's Aboriginals and other eligible voters, but the way that early 'white' Australia treated the right to vote of Australia's First People was a serious blot on Australia's otherwise exemplary history of electoral voting reform and took far too long to be resolved.

Australia was not the first to introduce many of the electoral systems discussed but was an early adopter of many electoral reforms. However, what may be more important than the extent of these reforms is their intent. From the early days of Federation, Australia was clear about its intentions. It understood the important institutional role of Australia's electoral processes. It was determined to introduce a broad electoral franchise, notwithstanding its early serious mistakes in this area. It would also do all it could to ensure that all eligible Australians participated in the electoral process, even to the extent of making it compulsory to do so. It introduced very early an electoral system that was as far as possible independent of party political processes and influence. And importantly, it accepted the mistakes it made in disenfranchising Australia's First Peoples, the Australian Aboriginals, and those of other ethnic backgrounds and eventually acknowledged and fixed these mistakes. In addition, Australia continues to strengthen its electoral processes and administration, and with it, strengthens the Australian polity, and the ability of the Australian polity to address the everchanging and complex political and economic challenges facing Australia. In that sense, Australia's electoral system is clearly part of Australia's second invisible hand.

Making a federation work – the Grants Commission[3]

It was just an arbitrary line on a map, running through the heart of a continent, 'the territory of New South Wales as including all the islands adjacent in the Pacific Ocean' and running westward to the 135th meridian, that is, about midway through the continent of Australia.[4] This was the directive given in 1787 to Captain Arthur Phillip by King George III (with the advice of his Privy Council), as he set off for the new colony of New South Wales as its Governor in Chief.[5]

Over the next 50 years came other decisions to create more arbitrary boundaries, mainly straight lines, crisscrossing a vast land that began the process of defining what is now the six States and two Territories that constitutes contemporary Australia. These arbitrary boundaries were determined in the late 18th and early 19th century by officials in the United Kingdom with relatively little knowledge and understanding of the interior geography of this great southern land. And these British officials certainly had no knowledge of the boundaries respected by the Australian Aboriginal and Torres Strait Islander peoples that were centred on intimate, personal and cultural relationships with the land and the sea.

And so was born an Australia and its colonies, based on lines of longitude and latitude that had no relationship with the underlying wealth or the expected needs of the people who would make their home within these boundaries. Nor could these early constructors of colonial Australia have understood just how troublesome these decisions would become on the early development of colonial Australia during discussions on whether Australia would become a federation, and how the challenges created by these uninformed decisions have remained, even until today. These decisions made over 240 years ago eventually created the need to establish organisations that could wrestle with the consequences of these early decisions.

The Commonwealth Grants Commission was eventually formed in 1933 to help find solutions to the consequences of these decisions made for Australia in the later part of the 18th century. Many nations have federal structures, and few nations have the same federal structure. Australia's federalism is not unusual amongst other federations; however, how Australia has decided to address the challenges of federation can truly be described as unique.

Australia is exceptional amongst federations in that it has attempted to simultaneously address two fundamental challenges of all federations. That is, how federations address any significant disparity between the State's revenue raising capabilities and how to address the different economic and social needs of these States. The first point is called vertical fiscal imbalance, and the second point is called horizontal fiscal equity. Since 1933, the organisation that the Commonwealth, the States and more recently the Territories has asked to advise on this matter is the Commonwealth Grants Commission.

With the great benefit of over 200 years of hindsight, it now seems obvious that once these arbitrary decisions about boundaries were made, Australia was always going to need an organisation something like the Commonwealth Grants Commission to help smooth out the very significant differences in the fiscal capabilities and the service needs of first the colonies, and then after federation, of the States of Australia that lay within these arbitrary boundaries.

Although the establishment of the Commonwealth Grants Commission is inextricably linked with the creation of the Commonwealth of Australia in 1901, they were not created in tandem. In the late 1800s, there were many discussions, debates, conventions and conferences across Australia about whether Australia should become a federation, and if so, how a 'commonwealth' of Australia would operate in principle and in practice. Throughout the national conversation in the latter part of the 19th century about whether Australia should federate, there was always a general acceptance of two essential principles if federation did eventuate.

First, that there would be free trade between the States (previously the colonies), and second, that the States would cede to the Commonwealth the right to impose customs and related excise duties (Commonwealth Grants Commission 1995, p. 1). This latter decision meant that at Federation, the States as a whole would lose control of a critically important source of revenue and independence, although it is not clear that the full implications of this reality were understood at the time.[6] Before federation, the colonies received three quarters of their revenue from customs and related excise duties (McLean 2004).

Not surprisingly, the reality of fiscal inequity between the former colonies was a central sticking point in their willingness to federate. The smaller and less wealthy colonies disliked the very idea of delegating significant financial power to a national government, which they feared would be dominated by the larger and more endowed colonies of New South Wales and Victoria. Moreover, unlike Canada, the Australian colonies were not sub-servient to a Federal Government and had both separate legislative power and direct access to the Crown (Prest 1967). They had to be won over by firm assurances that this matter would be adequately addressed, if federation was to proceed.

The colonial Premiers were finally convinced when, at the Premier's Conference of January 1899, the proposed Commonwealth Constitution was amended to ensure that the States would be provided with a fixed percentage of the Commonwealth's revenue from customs and excise duties for the first 10 years of the federation, and that the Commonwealth would have the power to grant financial assistance to the States if required. Little did the colonial Premiers realise at the time that the power of the Commonwealth to grant financial assistance to the States, an idea which was almost an afterthought at the 1898 Constitutional Convention would come to dominate future relations between the States and the Commonwealth (Commonwealth Grants Commission 1995, p. 4).

After much debate, and a few false starts, Federation in Australia occurred in 1901. Almost from the beginning of the Australian Federation, the per capita distribution of Commonwealth grants to the States was unequal and reflected not the financial and social needs of a State, but a State's contribution to Commonwealth customs revenue (Morris 2002). This had a substantial impact on the States, as by design, they were now heavily dependent on financial transfers from the Federal Government for the funding of their legislated responsibilities in education, health and law and order (Williams 2012, p. 146).

From the beginning of Federation, and until the establishment of the Commonwealth Grants Commission in 1933, the new Commonwealth Government struggled with how to manage the significant differences in the revenue raising capacity of the States, and the implication of this reality for the provision of State services, and the cohesion of the Federation as a whole. To attempt to address this imbalance and its consequences, from as early as 1910, the new Commonwealth allocated special grants to some states, starting with Western Australia, then followed Tasmania in 1912 and South Australia in 1931.

The reality of the uneven nature of the revenue raising nature of the States was brought into stark relief during the 1930s Great Depression when it was clearly revealed for all to see that there was a greater fiscal difference between States than was previously acknowledged and that this significantly curtailed the ability of some States to put in place even the most rudimentary services and support for those most seriously affected by the Great Depression (Morris 2002).

It wasn't that this nascent federation was oblivious to these concerns. From the time of Federation until the 1930s, the Commonwealth and the States had attempted to understand these legitimate concerns and how to address them through ad hoc enquiries and by reference to a variety of bodies and organisations. The first substantial review of Commonwealth financial assistance to the States was the 1924 Royal Commission on the Finances of Western Australia as Affected by Federation. Then closely following this review came the 'Special Investigation' by Sir Nicholas Lockyer into the financial position of Tasmania. Not surprisingly, in 1927, South Australia then set up its own Royal Commission into the effects of federation on its finances. In response to the South Australian review, the Commonwealth established its own Royal Commission on the Finances of South Australia as Affected by Federation. This Royal Commission completed its work in 1929. Then in 1930 came a series of Commonwealth Parliamentary reviews, one specifically targeting the financial position of Tasmania, and another into the generality of special grants to the States. Invariably and unsurprisingly, each of these reviews would find in favour of some additional and specific funding for whichever State was the subject of that particular review.

By 1926, suggestions began to emerge from several respected quarters for the establishment of some form of independent committee or body to advise the Commonwealth on how to best address the important issue of fiscal equalisation between the States (Commonwealth Grants Commission 1995).[7]

Lyndhurst Falkiner Giblin, a past Labor politician, former Tasmanian statistician and an early supporter of the Economics Society of Australia and New Zealand, was one of the first to seriously raise the idea of a permanent and independent body to advise the Commonwealth Parliament on matters of Commonwealth/State Financial matters. Giblin was also to become Ritchie Chair of Economic Research at University of Melbourne, and amongst other roles, a founding member of the Commonwealth Grants Commission. Others such as W K Hancock, Professor of History at the University of Adelaide, Sir William Harrison Moore, Emeritus Professor of Law at the University of Melbourne, T J Hytten, who was to become a professor of Economics at the University of Tasmania, and many Commonwealth politicians were by the early 1930s arguing forcefully for the establishment of an independent body to advise on Commonwealth/State financial matters.

By the early 1930s, support for a permanent and independent body to advise on the issue of Commonwealth/State financial matters, a matter seen as being critical to the ongoing success of the still young Federation, was becoming more widespread and politically acceptable, and seen as a sensible means to help overcome the ad hoc nature of the arrangements that were operating at the time.

A final catalyst for the establishment of an independent body to advise on this increasingly urgent dilemma was the 1933 Western Australian referendum, where the citizens of Western Australia were being asked whether they wished to secede from the Commonwealth. Western Australians voted by an almost two-thirds majority in favour of succession and the decision to establish an independent body to advise on financial grants to the States followed soon after.

Although it's convenient to link the eventual establishment of the Commonwealth Grants Commission to the results of this referendum, this might be a far too convenient explanation. It seems that Prime Minister Joseph Lyons may have had a long-standing preference for such a body, and the referendum may have been a catalyst, but not the reason for the eventual establishment of the Commission.[8]

The first Commissioner, Tasmanian Lyndhurst Falkiner Giblin, took an egalitarian view of its mandate (in the face of objections from his chairman). Both Giblin and a later Commissioner Russell Lloyd Matthews, an ANU Professor of Commerce originally from Geelong, believed that the

Commission's role to report on States' financial disabilities should be interpreted widely. Thus began the convention within the Commission that a State suffered a financial disability if its revenue capacity or cost of delivering services differed from the mean of the other States (McLean 2004). This broader ambit of the Commission's role has, over the years, not been without its critics who believe the Commission has been surreptitiously making the formula more egalitarian over the years without statutory warrant.

Although the specific methods the Commission has adopted to complete its task have changed over its life, the fundamental reason for its existence has remained constant. Its role, put simply, is to provide transparent, impartial, independent and objective advice to the Commonwealth Government on the financial resources required by each State and Territory to enable them to provide at a minimum, a generally accepted 'Australian average' level of services to their respective citizens, and the financial ability of the individual State or Territory to do so.

However, whereas the work of the Commission aims to provide the States and Territories with the fiscal capability to provide at a minimum this 'Australian average' level of service to its citizens, neither the Commonwealth Government, and certainly not the Commission compel them to do so. Nor does the Commonwealth or the Commission hold the States or the Territories accountable for their spending of the funds allocated to them because of Commission recommendations. The accountability in this regard remains firmly with the citizens of those individual States or Territories.

Not all nations operate as federations. Some nations, such as the UK, New Zealand and France, operate an unitary system, with one central government providing most of the essential services for all its citizens. Other nations, such as the USA and Canada, operate as federations with a central government and significant sub-central governments providing a range of services.

Many federations, just like Australia, have attempted to overcome the difficulties of ensuring some degree of equality in the delivery of services and infrastructure between sub-national jurisdictions. Federations understand the importance of this reality for the welfare of their citizens, because significant sub-national economic differences in economic well-being can quickly emerge if some form of national financial support is not available to these regions.

What seems to differentiate Australia's attempt to resolve this serious conundrum from other federations is:

- The ability of Australia to constantly and if required, urgently address the level of fiscal imbalances between the States and Territories as circumstances change.

- The willingness to address fiscal imbalances between the States and Territories by better understanding and accommodating both the overall contemporary needs of the citizens of the States and Territories, and a sophisticated understanding of their revenue raising capabilities and service delivery performance.
- The preparedness to establish an organisation that would provide impartial, independent and objective advice to the Commonwealth Government on these critical matters.

During the early years of the Commission, the States had the ability to levy their own income taxes. This revenue raising capability was ceded to the Commonwealth during World War II. In the early life of the Commission, because States had the ability to levy their own income taxes, its role was to consider the grants to be paid to what was described as the financially weaker, or, 'claimant States' of Western Australia, Tasmania and South Australia. As a result of the States ceding their income taxing powers to the Commonwealth, this led to the abolition of State income tax, and the introduction of uniform federal taxation arrangements. However, this wasn't without significant cost to the States, because, as a result, vertical fiscal imbalance increased. This then led to the introduction of tax reimbursement grants that sat alongside of additional grants to the claimant States. This was followed during the 1950s with further changes where grants to the States from the Commonwealth were distributed primarily based on their population. Further changes to Commonwealth financial allocation to States were again made in the late 1950s, and then again in the mid-1970s.

The introduction by the Coalition Howard Government of a Goods and Services Tax (GST) in 2001 was a very significant development for the States, and therefore for the Commission. In the decision to implement the GST, it was agreed that all GST revenues would be distributed to the States and Territories to replace several Commonwealth grants and with the agreement and understanding that the States would remove what was thought to be inefficient State-based taxes.

Having access to the revenues raised through the GST not only made the pool of allocated funds larger but given the use of a set formulae for the distribution of GST to the States and Territories, there was less scope for political tinkering with the financial allocations to the States and Territories.

Throughout its history, the Commission's approach has varied, for example to consider cost differences between the States, by considering the effect which extra per capita payments to the States by the Commonwealth might have on a State's ability to provide services and by taking into account specific State-based events such as fires and floods and even the level of urbanisation and socio-economic variables between States. The Commission has also grappled with the difficult question of how to best consider a State's revenue raising capacity resulting from its natural resource endowments, particularly its mineral resources (Commonwealth Grants Commission, 2020, p. XV).[9]

The willingness of the Commission to consult extensively with the States and Territories before it makes its recommendations has contributed to the Commission's continuing its important role in Commonwealth-State financial arrangements, policy and practices. However, it has not been the Commission alone which has enabled Australia's approach to effectively support the operation of the Australian Federation. The States and Territories have, over the years, become highly constructive contributors to the ongoing work of the Commission, and have supported Australia's general approach to horizontal fiscal equity, even though the public utterances of State treasurers and Premiers when the allocation of funding to the States is announced would lead the Australian population to think otherwise.

Although the contribution of the Commission to Commonwealth-State financial arrangements has varied over time, its influence has never changed. Without the willingness of the Commission to modify its approach to the provision of advice over the years to meet the changing economic circumstances of the States and Territories, and to do so in an objective, transparent and professional manner, the Commission may have become just another marginal player in the complex domain of Commonwealth-State relations. Decisions related to the provision of grants to the States would most likely have been determined on potentially divisive political grounds. Importantly, the Commonwealth Grants Commission has, from its inception, developed a reputation for both independence and competence.

The Australian Commonwealth Grants Commission differs significantly from similar organisations in other federations. The Organisation for Economic Cooperation and Development (OECD) makes clear that fiscal equalisation systems are 'tremendously country specific'[10] and that Australia is considered unique in the OECD as it has both horizontal and vertical fiscal equity components. McLean (2004) has argued that the Commission helps Australia achieve one of the highest degrees of horizontal fiscal equalisation to be found in any democratic federation. Having high horizontal fiscal equity ensures that States and Territories have the financial resources to ensure that all Australians have the opportunity to receive at a minimum, the 'Australian average' level of government provided services, no matter where they live in Australia.

Without question, the Commonwealth Grants Commission has for almost 90 years helped the effective and efficient working of the Australian Federation. In human terms, this means that if Australian governments heed the advice of the Commonwealth Grants Commission then all Australians, wherever they live in this vast land, can be confident that their respective State or Territory Government have at least the basic resources to provide them with at the very minimum of services equivalent to an 'Australian average' level of Government services, and a level of government services potentially commensurate with all other Australians. And for this, in large part, they can thank the ongoing, mostly unseen work of Australia's Commonwealth Grants Commission.

Notes

1 Thanks to comments from John Murphy.
2 The term the 'other invisible hand' is a term used by Mancur Olson to describe the economic benefits that arise from the constructive use of power in the social interest.
3 Sincere thanks to Professor Ross Williams, Dr Lynn William and Mr Greg Smith for their insightful and generous comments on this chapter.
4 www.foundingdocs.gov.au\item-did-35.html
5 www.foundingdocs.gov.au\item-did-35.html
6 The Constitution includes both principles as well as a protection for the independence of the States.
7 From the beginning of the Federation in 1901 until the establishment of the Commonwealth Grants Commission in 1933, several ad hoc approaches were tried to accommodate the inevitable challenges of this imbalance in the service delivery needs of the States and revenue raising capability of this new Commonwealth. These included proscribed allocation formulas, ad hoc revenue sharing arrangements and special grants to some states, and in particular, Western Australia, Tasmania and South Australia who since the beginning of the Federation had begun to establish significant grievances about the financial sharing arrangements of the new Federation (Commonwealth Grants Commission 1995).
8 Commonwealth Grants Commission (1995, p. 16).
9 Williams (2012, p. 149).
10 OECD (2007, p. 5).

References

Australian Bureau of Statistics, 1988. *1301.0 – Year Book Australia, 1988, History of Pensions and Other Benefits in Australia*, Archived Issue Released at 11:30 AM (Canberra Time), 1 January 1988, Australian Government, Canberra.

Australian Electoral Commission, 2019a. *A Short History of Federal Electoral Reform in Australia*, Australian Government, Canberra.

Australian Electoral Commission, 2019b. *Federal Election: Fast Facts*, Australian Government, Canberra.

Australian Electoral Commission, 2021, *Annual Report 2020–21,* Canberra, ACT.

Brennan, F., SJ, 2017. *The Legacy of Justice Higgins: Seeking a True New Start For All Job Seekers and Workers*, ACU, 8 November 2017 https://soundcloud.com/frank-brennan-6/rerum-novarum-oration-2017-the-legacy-of-justice-higgins-seeking-a-true-new-start-for-all-job-seekers-and-workers.

Brett, J., 2019. *From Secret Ballot to Democracy Sausage; How Australia Got Compulsory Voting*, The Text Publishing Company, Melbourne, Victoria.

Cameron, S. and McAllister, I., 2019a. *The 2019 Australian Federal Election: Results from the Australian Election Study*, Australian National University, Canberra.

Cameron, S. and McAllister, I., 2019b. *Trends in Australian Political Opinion: Results from the Australian Election Study, 1987–2019*, Australian National University, Canberra.

Commonwealth Grants Commission, 1995. *Equality in Diversity. History of the Commonwealth Grants Commission*, 2nd ed., Australian Government Publishing Service.

Commonwealth Grants Commission, 2020. *Report on GST Revenue Sharing Relativities 2020 Review – Volume 1*, Braddon, ACT. (http://www.cgc.gov.au).

Daniels, Dale, 2011. *History of Australian pensions*. Australian Parliament House, Posted 24 February 2011 by Dale Daniels, https://www.aph.gov.au/About_Parliament/Parliamentary_Departments/Parliamentary_Library/FlagPost/2011/February/History_of_Australian_pensions.

Dickey, Brian, 1980. *No Charity There: A Short History of Social Welfare in Australia*, Nelson, Melbourne, 1980, pp. 30–66; Stephen Garton, *Out of Luck: Poor Australians and Social Welfare, 1788–1988*, Allen & Unwin, Sydney, 1990, pp. 48–54.

Dixon, J., 1983. Australia's Income-security System: Its Origins, Nature and Prospects. *International Social Security Review*, 36(1), pp. 19–44.

Encel, S., 1996. Retirement Ages and Pension Ages – A Complex History. *Social Security Journal*, June 1996, Social Policy Research Centre, University of New South Wales, Sydney.

Ex Parte, HV McKay, 1907. *Commonwealth Arbitration Report Volume 2*, pp. 1–2, p. 4, p. 5, Melbourne.

Fair Work Australia, 2011. *Waltzing Matilda and the Sunshine Harvester Factory*, Fair Work Australia, Melbourne, p. 65.

Garton, Stephen, 2008. Health and Welfare. *The Dictionary of Sydney*, Online https://dictionaryofsydney.org/entry/health_and_welfare.

Hawke, R.J., 2010. *The Inaugural Bishop Manning Lecture*, Thursday 7 October 2010, Sydney, p. 2, p. 3.

Hennock, E.P., 2003. Social Policy in the Bismarck Era: A Progress Report. *German History*, 21, pp. 229–238.

Herscovitch, A. and Stanton, D., 2008. History of Social Security in Australia. *Family Matters*, 80, pp. 51–60.

International Institute for Democracy and Electoral Assistance, 2021. *Compulsory Voting*, www.idea.int/data-tools/data/voter-turnout/compulsory-voting

Kewley, T.H., 1973. *Social Security in Australia, 1900–72*, 2nd ed., Sydney University Press, Sydney, https://catalogue.nla.gov.au.

Kirby, Michael, 2004. *Industrial Conciliation and Arbitration in Australia – A Centenary Reflection*, Melbourne, Friday 22 October 2004, p. 7.

The Marine Cooks, Bakers, and Butchers' Association of Australia V the Commonwealth Steam-Ship Owners Association, 1907/08 2 CAR 55: p. 60, p. 61, Melbourne.

Kunze, N.L., 1971. *The origins of modern social legislation: The Henrician poor law of 1536*. Albion, 3(1), pp. 9–20.

Markwell, Donald J., 2000. Keynes and Australia. *Research Discussion Paper 2000–04, Research Department, Reserve Bank of Australia, and New College*, Oxford and Sydney, Reserve Bank of Australia.

McLean, I., 2004. Fiscal Federalism in Australia. *Public Administration*, 82(1), pp. 21–38.

Morris, A., 2002. The Commonwealth Grants Commission and Horizontal Fiscal Equalisation. *Australian Economic Review*, 35(3), pp. 318–324.

Murphy, J., 2008. The Poverty of Liberalism: The First Old Age Pensions in Australia. *Thesis Eleven*, 95(1), pp. 33–47.

Murphy, J., 2021. Social Protection and Vulnerability: Australia's Distinctive Public Policy Profile. In *The Oxford Handbook of Australian Politics*, edited by Jenny M. Lewis and Anne Tiernan, Print Publication Date. Oxford: Oxford University Press. http://doi.org/10.1093/oxfordhb/9780198805465.013.10.

OECD, 2007. *Fiscal Equalisation in OECD Countries*. Working Paper No 4. OECD, Paris.

Olson, M., 2000. *Power and Prosperity: Outgrowing Communist and Capitalist Dictatorships*, Basic Books, New York.

Plummer, A., 1927. Some Aspects of the History and Theory of Social Insurance. *Economica*, 20, pp. 203–223. http://doi.org/10.2307/2548429.

Prest, W., 1967. Federalism in Australia: The Role of the Commonwealth Grants Commission. *Journal of Commonwealth & Comparative Politics*, 5(1), pp. 3–18.

Productivity Commission, 2018. *Horizontal Fiscal Equalisation*, Productivity Commission Inquiry Report, No 88, 15 May 2018, Canberra.

Rickard, John, 2020. *Higgins, Henry Bournes (1851–1929*, Australian Dictionary of Biography, National Centre of Biography, Australian National University, http:/adb.anu/biography/Higgins-henry-bournes-6662/text11483, published first in hardcopy 1983, accessed online 5 February 2020.

Sawer, M., 2012. Andrew Fisher and the Era of Liberal Reform. *Labour History: A Journal of Labour and Social History*, 102, pp. 71–86.

Williams, Ross, 2012. History of Federal-State Fiscal Relations in Australia: A Review of the Methodologies Used. *The Australian Economic Review*, 45(2), pp. 145–157.

3   Post-WWII grand ideas

Co-innovation in agriculture – the RDCS[1]

Agriculture, mining and manufacturing are typically the high productivity sectors of developed economies and, in Australia, they are embedded in competitive market environments. Much of their productivity growth comes however, not only from the competitive behaviour within their own sector. It comes from other sectors of the economy such as R&D, extension and logistics *inter alia*. But what if these other sectors do not naturally develop and link to agriculture, through the market?

Enter collective action. By 1990, the Australian agricultural sector was comfortably serviced by a patchwork of partnership agencies which facilitated multilateral knowledge flows between farms, research institutes, government and extension services (Grant 2012).[2] These agencies, called R&D corporations, featured end-user directed invention and joint research-industry activities around innovation, marketing and commercialisation. In short, they were early exemplars of co-innovation.

Unlike many other areas of economic innovation, these R&D Corporations had a relatively smooth birth being a by-product of a socialist system of agricultural research and current economic thought. In Australia in the 19th century, landmark inventions in agriculture often came from canny, solitary inventors responding to their own need or that of a single farming voice. The seed drill,[3] stump-jump plough[4] and the grain stripper[5] were among these early but pivotal Australian inventions. But over time, as the process of invention became more sophisticated and expensive, it was harder for lone geniuses to successfully innovate. As observed by Alfred Whitehead, the greatest invention of the early 20th century was the invention of invention. New modes of invention were needed.

In the late 19th century, large manufacturing conglomerates began to establish their own applied research labs. In Germany, they appeared in the chemical industry (e.g. I G Farben, Bayer); in the USA they sprung up in

DOI: 10.4324/9781003244424-3

chemical and mechanical industries (e.g. Du Pont, Westinghouse, General Motors, Ford, General Electric, AT&T, Kodak and railway firms).[6] These were complemented by professional and technical organisations[7] that conducted meetings and published journals that served as clearinghouses for new knowledge and techniques.

The extensive fragmentation of the farming industry meant that there were few large industry champions that could profitably do this. A single company needed to shoulder the up-front costs of invention and garner enough of the innovation profits for the whole exercise to pay. This was difficult for most farms. Accordingly, governments stepped into the breach. In Australia, government involvement in agricultural research began in the 1850s when the Victorian Board of agriculture took over the first experimental farm that had been established by a farmers' committee.[8] In the US, a flurry of activity took place in the 1860s with the establishment of the Department of Agriculture, the Weather Bureau, National Bureau of Standards and the land grant universities (to teach practical agricultural skills among other things) (Lawrence 1980). By 1900, six Australian states had agricultural departments and four had agricultural colleges which emphasised development and extension work. By 1900, the first joint government – industry research facility, the Queensland Bureau of Sugar Experimentation had been created (Hastings 1977).[9]

The creation of public sector research bureaus for industrial benefit is not new. What characterised the Australian system was the permanent establishment of intermediators – the R&D Corporations – between research and end-users groups. R&D Corporations are independent legal entities that are governed by the industry sector they represent (e.g. wool, sugar, grain, meat etc.). Within these R&D Corporations industry defines the problem requiring a research or marketing solution; outsources research or marketing to an expert body and then uses training and translation services to ensure farmers know how to adjust their farming practices.[10] These activities are paid for by a compulsory industry levy which is matched (up to a cap) by public funds. An important objective in establishing the R&D Corporation model was to bring a stronger end-user focus to research decisions and encourage faster uptake of research outputs by farmers.

This constellation of attributes did not arrive overnight in Australia but evolved with the support of (some) farmers and (some) Australian politicians over 50 years. The first step was the acceptance by farmers of a compulsory levy on their sales to support various forms of agriculture research and development. Among the more influential political advocates were Prime Ministers Earle Page (Country Party), Sir John McEwen (National Party), Ben Chifley (Labor Party) and Bob Menzies (Liberal Party) as well as Ministers Reginald Pollard (Labor Party) and

Jack Hallam (Labor Party) and CSIRO scientist Sir William Ian Clunies Ross (Inall 2015). The levy regime was introduced in 1900 for the Bureau of Sugar Experiment Stations at the instigation of farmers. It was then followed by the creation of the Pastoral Research Trust in 1920; a wool promotion and research levy in 1936 and the Wheatgrowers' Soil Fertility Research Fund in 1954 (PC 2011). In 1936, at the request of the wool industry, the Government made its levy compulsory and in 1945 the Government contributed matching funds (Winslade 1999). This model remained until the mid-1980s, during which time similar schemes were introduced in other farming industries.

It was not however until the 1980s that the R&D agencies developed their modern co-innovation business model. In 1983, a new Hawke Labor Government, including a new minister for agriculture, John Kerin, arrived in Canberra. This new Government had a very clear economic consensus on what needed to be done in general economic terms, as well as in industry and agricultural policy. Significantly, Kerin had previously worked in the Bureau of Agricultural Economics, under the tutelage of Dr Geoff Miller, and was well-versed in agricultural economics. Kerin believed the agencies needed greater links with industry and more emphasis on commercial viability. He thought the research agenda was too heavily directed by researchers and convinced his Labor Party colleagues and the Australian Parliament to adopt a corporate model for research and development which would give the R&D Corporations more power and flexibility (Productivity Commission 2011; Inall 2015). One of the fundamental changes was the conversion of statutory authorities into industry-owned corporations.

Kerin had developed his rural policy before reaching his Ministerial post and there was minimal opposition to his policies by the (agrarian socialist) National Party which had dominated farm policy since the 1920s. His greatest opposition came from the Australian Government Finance and Treasury Departments who argued that it was cheaper for Australia to buy its R&D and ideas from overseas. However, Kerin understood that it was difficult to absorb R&D and know-how unless you had local research capability. Hence Kerin argued that outsourcing research to a body remote from the farming community was going to be a false economy. Kerin's view clashed with senior Government members such as Finance Minister Peter Walsh, who thought subsidies in their various forms merely encouraged rent-seeking behaviour, and with senior Government bureaucrats who Kerin argued did not understand that the ultimate beneficiary of agricultural R&D were consumers who got better and cheaper food (and agricultural materials). Fortunately for Kerin, Prime Minister Bob Hawke and his Cabinet were economically literate (e.g. Ralph Willis, Bill Hayden) and understood his arguments. The National Farmers' Federation gave quiet backing to many of these reforms and importantly, their lack of public disapproval of these initiatives was important in making way for their introduction.

One of the latent consequences of bringing agricultural producers together with the science community was a broadening of farmers' vision for what science could do for them. This did not occur overnight. Changing mindsets is difficult and some agricultural groups actively resisted change (Kerin 2017). To this end, Kerin ensured that the Chair of each agricultural R&D Corporation was scientifically qualified with the bulk of the members being industry appointed.

Remarkably, Kerin's reforms have now the support across the political spectrum and remain in place to the present (being the early 2020s).

Opening for business – dismantling import restrictions[11]

Economists and policy analysts have long struggled with the rationale for import tariffs. Tariffs have been used since ancient times as a source of government revenue, along with tolls on bridges, ports and transport routes. Their justification as policy instruments – to protect local industry from unfair competition – came later and was effectively bolted on ex post.

In the 18th century, philosophical discussions about the role of import restrictions whirled around Europe but the issue came to a fierce head in the 1830s over the British Corn Laws. Restrictions on the import of foreign corn (i.e. wheat) was thought to protect farm incomes but economic thought, as crisply analysed by David Ricardo, showed that they undermined food supply and largely bolstered the incomes of landlords.

Australia followed in this revenue-raising-cum-protectionist tradition, and tariffs on alcoholic beverages were introduced in 1800. Import tariffs were important revenue raising mechanisms for the Australian colonies leading up to the establishment of the Commonwealth of Australia in 1901.[12] Following World War I, a Tariff Board was established by the Commonwealth to review all requests for new import tariffs and quotas (Lloyd 2017; Corden 2005).

By the 1950s, Australia was the most protectionist country in the OECD, after New Zealand, with an average tariff rate of about 30%. However, by 2017, Australia had close to the lowest tariff rates in the world, with an average tariff of less than 1%. How did this come about?

Australia's journey to a low tariff environment was difficult, uneven and challenging for the many protected industry sectors. Tariff protection had become a default setting for many sectors with Ville and Merrett (2000) claiming that during the 19th century 'producers had only to ask to receive all manner of "protection" '(p. 26).[13]

The Australian journey to a low tariff environment was chiefly driven by the intellectual force of a small number of academic economists. It was eventually taken up by successive Australian governments which accepted the power of these intellectual arguments. The change was unilateral (i.e. done without reciprocity by trading partners) and this is unusual in the global trade context where reciprocity was and remains the dominant guiding principle for tariff cuts. The arguments were, in short, that Australia's high level of import tariffs were lowering the average standard of living of the Australian people, *regardless of tariffs imposed on its exports by other nations*.

In 1957, a young University of Melbourne economist, Max Corden published 'The Calculation of the Cost of Protection' in the *Economic Record*. In this article, Corden (1958) showed theoretically that Australian industries were disadvantaged by tariffs imposed on their imported inputs. As a corollary, he said the Tariff Board should re-think how tariffs were imposed. At the 1958 ANZAAS Annual Congress, he argued that the first gradual move towards reform should be to impose a uniform tariff rate. He eschewed wholesale changes as this would invoke massive shocks to the economy and incur short-term misery. The lecture made considerable impact and was fully reported in the media.

But changing a whole structure of explicit and hidden subsidies and taxes was going to take more than a convincing argument. There were strong vested interests in the existing structure of tariffs, and, as with most reforms, the beneficiaries of reform were thinly spread and generally unknowing of the potential benefits.

Corden (1958, 1962) took the view that to reform an institution you had to understand its own internal logic and there is always a logic behind every institution. For the tariff structure, the logic at the time was to ensure full employment for a growing population. Tariffs took the place of a decrease in the value of the Australian dollar and prevented business closures. However, it became the accepted practice at this time for the Tariff Board to be heavily lobbied by pecuniary interests and political pressures, not all of which were clearly aligned with the goal of full employment. The Board needed an independent and impartial ally.

A turning point in Australia's highly protectionist approach to industrial development came with the appointment of Alf Rattigan as the new head of the Tariff Board. Alf Rattigan was appointed in 1963 to be the head of the Tariff Board by the protectionist Minister of Trade, John McEwen, in the belief that he, Rattigan, would be a compliant insider that would continue to support Australia's protectionist policies. However, Rattigan turned out to be a progressive reformer on a mission and he was looking for a rationale to re-think tariff policy.

In 1963, the Vernon Committee was established by the Menzies Government, in part, at the suggestion of ANU academic John Crawford, a prominent local figure and former Secretary to the Department of Trade (Vernon 1965). For this Committee, Corden was asked to calculate actual effective rates of protection facing various industries. Effective rates consider the disadvantage to a business from tariffs on its inputs as well as the advantage from tariffs on competing finished products. These effective-rate-of-protection estimates were the first to be made anywhere in the world and were taken up with gusto by Rattigan (who became inaugural chairman of the Industries Assistance Commission (IAC), the successor to the Tariff Board) and his colleague Bill Carmichael (who became a subsequent Chairman of the IAC in the 1980s). While a staff member on the Tariff Board, Carmichael was the driving force behind running the effective-rate-of-protection ruler over business requests for more tariffs.

But all this was ad hoc and time consuming. The real issue was how to dismantle the whole system. This required economists to first convince key political figures that low trade barriers was more conducive to full employment than the existing complex web of tariffs, and second to establish that there was a feasible way to achieve this without structural dislocation and (temporary) high rates of business closure and the resulting unemployment. Manufacturers felt they had much to lose from tariff reductions and were a powerful lobby group especially within the Labor Party which had a traditional constituency in the manufacturing workforce and the trade unions that represented them.

A mark of the impact academic economists had on shifting people's views around trade policy was the revolving door between town and gown. In the mid-1960s, Max Corden, Fred Gruen, Alan Powell, Garry Pursell and Richard Snape worked with the Tariff Board to develop a proper economic framework for tariff-making, in the face of staunch opposition from the Government. During the Whitlam years, Richard Snape was part of a review to bring fresh analytical insights in trade policy for the benefit of the Prime Minister and his Cabinet. He was at various times consultant and employee and commissioner of the Industries Assistance Commission, the Industry Commission, the Productivity Commission, UNCTAD and the World Bank. During the 1970s, academic economists Alan Powell, Peter Dixon and Richard Snape were supported by the Industries Assistance Commission to build the ORANI model, a computerised, applied, general equilibrium model to put numbers on resource distortions caused by the tariff structure. Future Prime Minister and then head of the union movement, Bob Hawke entered the fray along with Ross Garnaut when they were both appointed by Prime Minister Malcolm Fraser to the Crawford Committee's review of structural adjustment of manufacturing industries in 1978. These academics also understood the power of the media – especially the *Australian Financial Review* – for putting economic debates on the map.

Academics were not the only interested parties in this national and hotly contested debate. For example, Bert Kelly, a farmer and Liberal Member of the Commonwealth Parliament for the South Australian electorate of Wakefield from 1958 until 1977 was a central figure in creating a popular mandate for dismantling Australia's tariff walls. His father, Stan Kelly was a life-long opponent of protection because of what he described as its corrupting effect on politics and the unfair and unequal economic distributional effects that import tariffs had on the Australian community and in particular on the Australian agricultural sector. Bert Kelly continued with his father's campaign against import tariffs by not only consistently arguing against them in the Australian Parliament, but also through his biting criticism and tongue in cheek articles in the *Australian Financial Review* about Australia's protectionism.[14]

An entree to senior political figures was critical if Australia was to begin to reduce its import tariffs. On the advice of ANU economist, Fred Gruen, the reformist Labor Prime Minister Gough Whitlam reduced tariffs across the board by 25% in 1973. Even though Whitlam was what he described as a Rattigan man, there was no consensus within his party about the need to reduce tariffs and considerable tensions existed between the Treasurer, Jim Cairns, and Whitlam. As a result, many 'temporary' assistance measures including quotas were put in place in 1974 to 1975 for steel, motor vehicles and the Textiles, Clothing and Footwear industries *inter alia*. This was largely to counter a sudden rise in unemployment at the time. The sudden large 25% cut (which was really intended to cut inflation) arguably undermined political appetite for further cuts for over a decade. But as Whitlam's Government was cut short after only 3 years, the transformation to a low tariff environment stalled.

The final move by Australia to a low tariff environment came with the election of the Bob Hawke Labor Government in 1983. Here again, the journey to a low tariff environment was uneven, and required not only an intellectual understanding of the benefits and costs of lower tariffs but learning from the experience of the Whitlam Labor government, it recognised that it needed a practical and equitable means of getting there. In this regard the role of the leadership of Australia's Union movement was central to the final move to a low tariff environment. In that regard the leaders of the Australian Council of Trade Unions (ACTU), including Simon Crean, Bill Kelty and Martin Ferguson were critically influential in helping the union movement understand these issues and helping the Hawke/Keating Labor Government design the support required for displaced workers resulting from changes in industry protection (Snape, Gropp and Luttrell 1998).

By the 1980s, the broad arguments about the value to Australia of unilaterally dismounting trade barriers was largely accepted by both major political parties and the labour movement and hence there was no substantial

political push for policy reversal. The main opponents to reducing Australia's highly protectionist stance were the NSW Labor right and the Business
Council of Australia who voiced their members' fear of change. However,
the National Farmers Federation and the Australian Mining Industry Council eventually understood the (positive) implications for their exporting con-
stituencies of trade liberalisation and exerted their muscle (Garnaut 1994).

The Hawke/Keating Labor Government began their first term in office in
1983 with industry sector plans to reform Australia's most protected industries at the time – the passenger motor vehicle, textile, clothing and footwear,
shipbuilding, heavy engineering and the steel industry. This was overseen
by Senator John Button, the incoming Industry Minister. The most complex
of these industry plans was the plan for the passenger motor vehicle industry
which became known as the Button Car Plan. John Button's engaging and
empathetic relationship with various sectors of the passenger motor industry, combined with Bob Hawke's acumen and style in bringing the public
along with change and reform was critical. Hawke believed it was important not to surprise people and made a point of socialising future reforms
by frequently airing issues in his speeches. According to Garnaut (1994),
Hawke's style was to have intensive public discussion about reforms, led by
the Government but leveraging the support of vested interest groups within
society. There was also a sense that the Government was responding to an
economic crisis.

John Button was to become Australia's longest serving Industry Minister,
and through his commitment, political skill and quirky, but likable personal-
ity, was central to the success of the Hawke/Keating Governments' plans to
reduce import tariffs to historically low levels.

In 1988, under the advice of ANU economist Ross Garnaut and the
Industry Commission, Labor Prime Minister, Bob Hawke, set out a plan
for a phased reduction in quotas and the nominal tariff rate for most industries. This signalled a shift in Government strategy from industry specific
restructuring plans to general import tariff reductions. Under this new
approach, all industry sectors would see reductions in import tariffs to
10% or 15%, except for the passenger motor vehicle sector and the textile,
clothing and footwear sectors which were still subject to their own specific
restructuring plans.

Again, in 2008, the Labor government, under the auspices of the Bracks
and Green Reviews,[15] completed Australia's planned move away from
import tariffs as the main support to industries by further reducing general
import tariffs to a general rate of 5%. This was alongside programs for
the orderly exit of inefficient businesses and the pivot to championing
those businesses who were committed to increased scale, innovation and
exports.

Although this didn't mean the end of government assistance to industry, it did end a form of highly selective, discretionary and costly government assistance that had been in place in Australia for almost 90 years.

Medicines for all – the PBS[16]

Australia was one of the first countries to establish a universal pharmaceutical scheme. The initial scheme which began in 1948 subsidised the price consumers paid for a group of medicines for a limited group of Australians and used Australia's buying power to lessen patentees' monopoly power. It was the start of a new era in population health in Australia. The prospect of loss of life during World War II led directly to massive investment into the development of Alexander Fleming's antibiotics (led by London-based Australian Howard Florey and German Ernst Chain). In the process, it lifted drugs and chemical cures to a significantly higher scientific footing (Malerba and Orsenigo 2015). Penicillin was a wonder drug which provided an immediate cure for bacterial infections that had hitherto caused death among young, healthy and otherwise robust people. This drug, and others such as streptomycin to treat tuberculosis, were beyond the financial means of many people. The outcry over this injustice caught the attention of progressive social reformers (Goddard 2014).

The Australian Labor Government, led by John Curtin, had a vision. In 1941, the Commonwealth Parliament set up committees to report how to improve health services for all Australians (Sloan 1995). By February 1944, Curtin began to legislate for universal free provision of pharmaceuticals under which all Australian residents would be entitled to free drugs from a limited prescribed list. War and peace had become the catalyst for a new society that could be fairer and more efficient than before. It was the age of grand ideas.

Globally, government incursion into subsidising pharmaceuticals had been growing since the late 19th century but coverage had always been selective. Bismarck's world-first government health insurance scheme, introduced in 1883, only provided free medicine for low-income workers (Goddard 2014). In 1911, Britain introduced limited national health insurance to cover the cost of pharmaceuticals for workers, but not their dependents (Light 2003). Free pharmaceuticals had been available in Australia since 1919, under the aegis of the Repatriation Pharmaceutical Benefits Scheme, but only for ex-service men and women (Sloan 1995; Biggs 2003).

Curtin's 1944 attempt at universality failed. The Australian Branch of the British Medical Association (BMA) successfully challenged his Bill – twice – as unconstitutional. Nonetheless, after twice amending the Constitution, the Pharmaceutical Benefits Act 1947 was passed and the

Pharmaceutical Benefits Scheme (PBS) began operating on July 1, 1948. However, organised resistance by the medical profession meant that only 2% of doctors participated in the scheme even though it meant denying their patients access to free medicines (Hunter 1965).

This curious resistance from the medical association may be partly explained by the dominance of surgeons in the medical associations. It was a turf war over control and money. The BMA believed that funding should be spent on boosting surgery not drugs. According to Goddard (2014), the foremost voice of surgeons revealed the weak state of the pharmaceutical industry and relative powerlessness of physicians. Although we note that many physicians, at the time, were paid for dispensing medicines and their revenues could have been compromised by the proposed public scheme. According to Hunter (1965), surgeons feared that governments would dictate their conditions of work and rob them of their agency to set prices. Part of the resistance was also the affront of not being consulted first and the question of who would administer the system. Regardless, the public arguments were decidedly emotional, and the proposed scheme was labelled 'socialist interference' in what should be a private matter between the physician and his or her patient.

Labor lost power in December 1949. A few weeks later, Sir Earle Page (a former surgeon), was sworn in as Health Minister under a Menzies Liberal-Country Party Coalition Government and began reducing Labor's comprehensive scheme to a safety net only for pensioners and their dependents (Sloan 1995). Hospitals, which had been using Labor's comprehensive scheme, were not happy and by 1953, the scheme was extended once more to all Australian residents. According to Hunter (1965) the range of benefits offered in the Labor and later Liberal schemes were virtually indistinguishable.

The 1944 Curtin proposal was not the first attempt to introduce a comprehensive pharmaceutical scheme in Australia. In 1938, the United Australia Party, under the leadership of Joseph Lyons, had tried but failed due to opposition from doctors, trade unions, the Labor opposition, the Country Party, farmers and small business (Goddard 2014). Absurdly, some of the 1938 proponents were later opponents of Curtin's 1944 scheme but then later architects of the comprehensive 1953 scheme. According to Goddard, part of the issue between Labor and the BMA was lack of confidence and willingness to consult and share control over decisions. The Liberals, on the other hand, had a closer working relationship with the BMA and were prepared to compromise and insert relatively meaningless qualifiers into the legislation, such as that doctors will not be 'conscripted' into the system. At the time, this was quite an emotionally charged issue, which is ironic, given the current day privilege of owning a Medicare Provider number.

What was most radical about the Australian scheme was not so much the provision of subsidies to consumers but the flexing of Australia's collective buying power (Duckett 2004). Instituting a national scheme meant there were two prices in the market: the price the consumer paid and the price the producer received. Whenever prices to consumers are negligible or deferred (as in the case of prescribed drugs and student loans), the demand curve shifts right, and producers, with some market power, can obtain higher profit margins. As patents give pharmaceutical manufacturers considerable market power, the appropriate economic policy is to use one's national monopsony power to moderate this monopolistic effect.[17]

Almost from the start, the Department of Health sought to control producer prices, but the problem was that manufacturers had all the information on costs and the Department had none (Sloan 1995).[18] By 1963, the Minister for Health, HW Wade, was so concerned with the Department's inability to negotiate reasonable prices that he established a bureau, which included finance staff, to oversee the process for determining target prices. According to Sloan (1995), this was largely successful and over the next few decades the Government of the day instituted over 16 reviews and set up several new agencies to keep producer prices at an acceptable level (e.g. the Pharmaceutical Benefits Pricing Bureau, Parliament joint committees, the Ralph Inquiry, Generic Pricing Policy, the Industries Assistance Commission inquiries, Bureau of Industry Economics reports, Pharmaceutical Benefits Pricing Authority, Minimum Pricing Policy).

There is clear evidence that use of monopsony power in Australia successfully contained costs. The Australian government did not set prices per se but set the subsidy it would give to certain drugs. Without this subsidy, the market for the particular drug in Australia would be severely curtailed. Successive studies have found that producer prices for certain pharmaceutical products in Australia are considerably below most other developed countries (Industry Commission 1996; Productivity Commission 2001; Bureau of Industry Economics 1991; Jacobzone 2000; Löfgren 1998; OECD 2008; Sweeny 2002; Lopert and Henry 2002; Doran 2008; Duckett and Banerjee 2017; Duckett 2018). National governments have considerable leverage. Being listed on a consumer subsidy scheme, like the PBS, provides a manufacturer with a large market.

Australia continued to change its price setting institutions in relation to certain pharmaceutical products and in 1988 was first-in-the-world to use economic analysis (called a pharmaco-economic assessment) to identify the most efficient drugs for selection into a publicly funded formulary.[19] This system was designed and improved by many individuals, with notable contributions from David Evans, David Henry, Andrew Mitchell and Ruth Lopert. The Pharmaceutical Benefits Advisory Committee actively guided industry on how to make evidence-based submissions. Manufacturers had to make a submission to the Committee on the effectiveness of their drug and the Committee would then advise the Government on whether it was cost-effective at the proposed price. Importantly, this independent committee had the power of pre-veto and made recommendations that the minister inevitably followed.

This method worked to keep down the buying costs of major drug classes such as new anti-depressants, anti-hypertensives, gastric acid suppressants and cholesterol lowering agents. The cost minimisation approach meant that a patented drug that could not show an advantage over other drugs in head-to-head trials had to sell at the same price as the cheapest like product. Recommendations, however, were heavily contested. David Henry was the main driver trying to keep prices low, along with Don Birkett and later Martyn Goddard. They arguably saved the PBS many billions of dollars using this method but earned the ire of the Australian Pharmaceutical Manufacturers Association. Monopsony power is not without its limitations and the pharmaceutical industry had long argued that resulting low prices are a disincentive to domestic investment in manufacturing and research.

A Coalition Government was returned to power in 1996. Their health minister, Michael Wooldridge, supported the manufacturers' position and in 2001 appointed a former head of the manufacturers' lobby to the Committee. This led to 10 of the 12 Committee members resigning. Nonetheless, by the early 2000s, most OECD countries were using this pharmaco-economic assessment in their pricing decisions to varying degrees (Lopert and Henry 2002). Once large numbers of generic drugs entered those markets, the formula was not as cost minimising as the aggressive generic pricing policies achieved by other countries. The pricing system had the unintended consequence of maintaining prices at a high level even after prices fell due to generics entering the market. Australia's solution – of asking generic manufacturers what price they wanted – was not wholly effective. Nonetheless, the pharmaco-economic assessment method was an important innovation for its time and Australia is today the only jurisdiction in the world where an independent body has the power to pre-veto a drug.

History matters (Wilsford 1994). Instituting a universal pharmaceutical benefits scheme in the 1940s, when there were few essential drugs that were generally affordable, enabled the various stakeholders in the health system to improve and refine the institutions and systems for optimising the purchase and distribution of more and more significant drugs. Were Australia to introduce a managed pharmaceutical scheme today the cost and embedded practices within the health system would make that task herculean.

Notes

1 Thanks to valuable comments from Neil Inall, Tom Spurling and John Kerin.
2 Extension services are those services that take the mature and ready-to-use research finding to the farmer.
3 Jethro Tull invented the drill seed, in about 1733, for his own farm.
4 In 1878, the South Australian Government offered a prize for the invention that would enable farmers to plough lands which had many embedded obstacles such as stumps. Richard Bowyer Smith won with the stump-jump plough.
5 In1843, the South Australian corn exchange committee offered a prize of £40 to an approved plan for a grain reaper. John Ridley, a miller and wheat farmer, invented the highly successful reaper and not only declined to patent his machine, but refused all suggestions of reward.
6 Usselman (2013).
7 mechanics institutes
8 The Philosophical society of Australia was formed in 1821 and the Agricultural Society was established in the 1820s but was short-lived.
9 Established to enhance the productivity of the sugar industry by improving production methods and increasing the number and diversity of sugar cane products. At the same time, state and federal agricultural ministers were also focussed on price stabilisation schemes and subsidies on inputs such as fertilisers.
10 There is some oversight by government. Individual agreements with R&D Corporations outline what is expected of them in terms of performance, transparency and accountability.
11 Grateful thanks to Max Corden, Lisa Gropp, Peter Lloyd and Ross Garnaut for very valuable comments.
12 With the establishment of the Commonwealth, the newly formed States agreed to cede to the Commonwealth the power to impose import tariffs.
13 Ville and Merrett said that businesses 'operated in a negotiable environment in which competitive pressures were mediated by government intervention and regulation' and that 'Business people boldly defended their behaviour by asserting that competition was "wasteful" ' (2000, p. 27).
14 This was first in various agricultural journals under the pseudonym of 'Dave's Diary', and then most famously in the *Australian Financial Review* from 1969 until 1977 as 'A Modest Member'. When he lost preselection for the seat of Wakefield in 1977, he wrote as 'A Modest Farmer'.
15 Led by the Hon Steve Bracks and Professor Roy Green respectively.
16 Grateful thanks to Stephen Duckett, Martyn Goddard, David Henry, Kim Sweeny, Ruth Lopert and Andrew Mitchell.
17 According to Malerba and Orsenigo (2015) the 1946 US Patent Office decision to grant a patent to streptomycin set the precedent for patenting for pharmaceuticals and other naturally occurring substances.
18 The UK's Voluntary Price Regulation Scheme began in 1956 (Collier 2007).
19 It became mandatory in 1993. NICE was established after the Australian scheme.

References

Biggs, A., 2003. *The Pharmaceutical Benefits Scheme an Overview*, E-Brief: Online Only issued 16 September 2002; updated 13 November 2002; 29 November 2002; 2 January 2003 Amanda Biggs, Information/E-links, Social Policy Group, www.aph.gov.au/About_Parliament/Parliamentary_Departments/Parliamentary_Library/Publications_Archive/archive/pbs.

Bureau of Industry Economics 1991. The Pharmaceutical Industry: Impediments and Opportunities, *Program Evaluation Report 11*, AGPS, Canberra.

Collier, J., 2007. The Pharmaceutical Price Regulation Scheme. *British Medical Journal*, 334(7591), pp. 435–436.

Corden, W.M., 1957. The Calculation of the Cost of Protection. *Economic Record*, 33(64), pp. 29–51. Reprinted in abridged form in Corden, *The Road to Reform*. Addison-Wesley, South Melbourne, 1997, pp. 8–30.

Corden, W.M., 1958. Import Restrictions and Tariffs: A New Look at Australian Policy. *Economic Record*, 34(69), pp. 331–346. Reprinted as 'The Case for a Uniform Tariff' in Corden, *The Road to Reform*, Addison-Wesley, South Melbourne, 1997, pp. 31–46.

Corden, W.M., 1962. The Logic of Australian Tariff Policy. In *Planned and Unplanned Development* (Economic Papers No. 15), Economic Society of Australia and New Zealand, Sydney, pp. 38–58. Reprinted in abridged form in Corden, The Road to Reform, South Melbourne: Addison-Wesley, 1997, pp. 47–58.

Corden, W.M., 2005. Effective Protection and I. *History of Economics Review*, 42(1), pp. 1–11.

Doran, E. and Henry, David Alexander, 2008. Australian Pharmaceutical Policy: Price Control, Equity, and Drug Innovation in Australia. *Journal of Public Health Policy*, 29(1), pp. 106–120.

Duckett, Stephen, 2004. Drug Policy Down Under: Australia's Pharmaceutical Benefits Scheme. *Health Care Financing Review*, Spring, 25(3).

Duckett, Stephen, 2018. Expanding the Breadth of Medicare: Learning from Australia. *Health Economics, Policy and Law (2018)*, 13, pp. 344–368. © Cambridge University Press.

Garnaut, R., 1994. Australia. In *The Political Economy of Policy Reform*, edited by John Williamson, Institute for International Economics, Washington, DC, pp. 51–72.

Goddard, Martyn S., 2014. How the Pharmaceutical Benefits Scheme Began. *Medical Journal of Australia*, 201(1), pp. S23–S25.

Grant, A., 2012. Australia's Approach to Rural Research and Development and Extension. In *OECD (2012) Improving Agricultural Knowledge and Innovation Systems: OECD Conference Proceedings*, OECD Publishing, Paris.

Hastings, T., 1977. *The Economics of Public Sector Scientific Research in Australian Agriculture*, Master thesis, Adelaide: University of Adelaide.

Hunter, T., 1965. Pharmaceutical Benefits Legislation, 1944–50. *Economic Record*, 41, pp. 412–425.

Inall, N.J., 2015. *The Legacy of John Kerin: A Labor Party Man of Rural Policy Based on Science*, PhD thesis, Sydney: Western Sydney University.

Industry Commission, 1996. *The Pharmaceutical Industry*, Australian Government Publishing Service, Melbourne.

Jacobzone, S., 2000. *Pharmaceutical policies in OECD countries: Reconciling social and industrial goals*. Paris: Organisation for Cooperation and Development.

Kerin, J., 2017. *The Way I Saw It; The Way It Was: The Making of National Agricultural and Natural Resource Management Policy*, Analysis & Policy Observatory (APO), Melbourne.

Lawrence, G., 1980. Agribusiness: The American Example and Its Implications for Australia. *The Journal of Australian Political Economy*, 7, p. 41.

Light, Donald W., 2003. Universal Health Care: Lessons From the British Experience. *American Journal of Public Health*, 93(1), pp. 25–30. http://doi.org/10.2105/ajph.93.1.25.

Lloyd, P., 2017. The First 100 Years of Tariffs in Australia: The Colonies. *Australian Economic History Review*, 57(3), pp. 316–344.

Löfgren, H., 1998. The Pharmaceutical Benefits Scheme and the Shifting Paradigm of Welfare Policy. *Australian Health Review*, 21(2), pp. 111–123.

Lopert, Ruth and Henry, David, 2002. The Pharmaceutical Benefits Scheme: Economic Evaluation Works . . . But Is Not a Panacea. *Australian Prescriber*, 25(6).

Malerba, Franco and Orsenigo, Luigi, 2015. The Evolution of the Pharmaceutical Industry. *Business History*, pp. 1–24.

OECD, 2008. *Pharmaceutical Pricing Policies in a Global Market, OECD Health Policy Studies*, Organisation for Economic Cooperation and Development, Paris.

Productivity Commission, 2001. *International Pharmaceutical Price Differences*, Research Report, AusInfo, Canberra.

Productivity Commission, 2011. *Rural Research and Development Corporations*, Report No. 52, Final Inquiry Report, Productivity Commission, Canberra.

Sloan, Clyde, 1995. *A History of the Pharmaceutical Benefits Scheme 1947 to 1992*, Department of Human Services and Health, Canberra.

Snape, R.H., Gropp, L. and Luttrell, T., 1998. *Australian Trade Policy 1965–1997: A Documentary History*, Sydney: Allen and Unwin.

Sweeny, K., 2002. *Demand and Price Dynamics in Pharmaceutical Markets: Some International Comparisons*. Equity, Sustainability and Industry Development, Working Paper Series, Working Paper No. 11, Melbourne: Centre for Strategic Economic Studies, Victoria University of Technology.

Usselman, S.W., 2013. *Research and Development in the United States since 1900: An Interpretive History, School of History, Technology, and Society Georgia Institute of Technology*, Economic History Workshop, Yale University, file:///C:/Users/emwebster/OneDrive%20-%20Swinburne%20University/CTI/Economic%20innovations/usselman_paper.pdf November 11, 2013. Reprinted in Oxford Encyclopedia of the History of Technology in the United States.

Vernon, J., et al., 1965. *Report of the Committee of Economic Enquiry, Volume II*, Commonwealth of Australia, Canberra: AGPS.

Ville, S. and Merrett, D., 2000. The Development of Large Scale Enterprise in Australia, 1910–64. *Business History*, 42(3), pp. 13–46.

Wilsford, David, 1994. Path Dependency, or Why History Makes It Difficult But Not Impossible to Reform Health Care Systems in a Big Way. *Journal of Public Policy*, 14, pp. 251–283.

Winslade, S.L., 1999. *Establishing a Science-based National Innovation System for the Wool Industry 1930s – 1950*, https://rune.une.edu.au/web/bitstream/1959.11/6636/4/open/SOURCE06.pdf.

4   The baby-boomer reforms

Independent policy advice – the Productivity Commission[1]

Economic eggheads and academic boffins: unrealistic recommendations from an out-of-touch organisation. These are some of the politer views of the leadership, staff and work of Australia's Productivity Commission, particularly from those who might be disadvantaged by Productivity Commission recommendations.

The Australian Productivity Commission is an independent advisor to the Australian Government on diverse regulatory, economic, social and environmental matters. It is increasingly an organisation that other nations seek to emulate. The Commission conducts Commonwealth Government requested inquiries; produces performance reports on a range of government services; conducts investigations and produces research on competitive neutrality issues; undertakes self-directed research; presents on its work to conferences; and where appropriate, makes submissions to other government reviews and inquiries.[2] The scope of its work now traverses the whole of the Australian economy including social policy, government services, regulatory policy, environmental policy and services, the adequacy of services to Australia's indigenous peoples and matters central to the productivity of organisations in the public, private and not-for-profit sectors.

Some of the Commission's more recent inquiries and reviews covered Australia's superannuation System; the National Disability Insurance System; the Murray-Darling Basin Plan; the Economic Regulation of Airports; the potential for Reforms to Australia's Human Services, in addition to the regular assessments of the level of assistance to Australian industry and Australia's productivity performance.

The Economist, in its 25 October 2018 edition[3] examined what was sometimes described as the Australian economic miracle of over 25 years of continuous economic growth. *The Economist* highlighted Australia's pre COVID economic performance of an extended period of strong economic performance, its relatively low public debt, its affordable welfare state, its

DOI: 10.4324/9781003244424-4

popular support for mass migration and Australia's broad consensus on the policies underpinning these successes. These are areas of critical public interest and policy where the work of the Commission and its predecessors has been, and remains, highly influential.

Today's Productivity Commission emerged from the Australian Tariff Board which was established in 1921 (earlier names were the Industries Assistance Commission and Industry Commission). The Tariff Board was established to assist governments to resolve what has been a constant theme in Australia since the time of Federation – the bitter disputes between protectionists and free traders. At its inception, the Tariff Board was decidedly pro protection. In 1924, one of the four members of the newly established Tariff Board made very clear his position. "*We are non-partisan because we have been selected by a Government of a country, 95% of whose representatives are protectionists. We are four protectionists – God helping us, and you will add, God helping our country*".[4]

This pro protection stance of the Tariff Board changed over time as the evidence of the damage caused to the Australian economy by protection mounted. Importantly, the Tariff Board lacked an important set of legislative protections that only became available to its successors as a result of a recommendation by Sir John Crawford to the incoming Whitlam Labor Government in 1972. Crawford recommended that the new commission be given responsibility for regularly reporting on the level of protection and its cost to the community and that all important correspondence between the Government and this new commission be published. Crawford demanded independence, transparency and an economy-wide view as the operating principles for any replacement of the Tariff Board.

Notwithstanding the motivations of governments of various political persuasions, many of these principles and practices have ensured that integrity was handed down from one organisation to the next, as the Tariff Board morphed into todays Productivity Commission. Importantly, many of the leaders of these various organisations have moved with them as they transmogrified from one structure or focus to another. For example, Alf Rattigan led the Tariff Board in the 1960s and in the 1970s was to be the first Chair of the replacement to the Tariff Board, the Industries Assistance Commission. Bill Carmichael, a senior public servant with the Tariff Board while Rattigan was Chair, was to become the Chair of the Industries Assistance Commission. Gary Banks, a senior member of staff of the Industries Assistance Commission was to become an Executive Commissioner with the Industry Commission, effectively its Deputy Chair, and the inaugural Chair of the Productivity Commission where he served with distinction for 14 years.

There has similarly been an important consistency within the organisational structure and the staffing of these organisations as they changed their names and focus. In the 1960s, Rattigan established the Development Branch within the organisational structure of the Tariff Board to critically examine and scrutinise the Tariff Board's approach to its work.[5] The Development Branch, albeit some-times under different names, and often colourfully described internally within these various organisations as the 'thought police' has remained an important element of all predecessors to the Productivity Commission. Bill Carmichael was initially the leader of this important research arm of the Tariff Board. Over its 50-year history, many of the same people lead and contributed to the work of this group and were somehow able to help to ensure that the critical success factors – independence, transparency and taking a community-wide focus – were successfully transferred from organisation to organisation. Similarly, there was a remarkable loyalty and consistency amongst staff leading and organising the public enquiry processes and conducting the Commission's research. The transfer of knowledge and culture by these individuals from one organisation to another as they were established and developed should not be underestimated when considering the quality of the work, and the important role that today's Productivity Commission plays in Australian public policy debates.

Of course, not everybody agrees, nor should everybody agree with every utterance of the Productivity Commission. No organisation is infallible, par-ticularly when it comes to matters as complex as modern public policy, nor is the Productivity Commission infallible in this regard. So polarised opin-ions of its work are something that the Productivity Commission accepts and is well accustomed to.

In 1968, John McEwen, the Minister for Trade in the Gorton coalition Government made his views perfectly clear when describing the quality of the members of the Board of one of the predecessors of the Commission, the Tariff Board.

'If the Government were to be powerfully influenced by recommenda-tions (by the Tariff Board) on such critically important economic consider-ations, we would most certainly wish that advice to come from people of the highest standing and competence.' – 'In selecting members of the Board the Government has never looked for great eminence in economics or in other fields. Indeed, the conditions, including emoluments, of Board members are not aimed at attracting such people'.[6]

In the context of the times, John McEwen was probably right. At that time, the role of the Tariff Board, as understood by some Members of the Government of the day, including John McEwen, was simply to advise Gov-ernments about how high an import tariff needed to be to ensure an industry was able to compete with imports. For that role, Governments didn't see the need to hire the intellectually adventurous.

Over 50 years on from the days of the Tariff Board, and while the echoes of the opinions of McEwen are still sometimes heard, Australia's Produc-tivity Commission today remains one of the Australian Government's key advisors, staffed by some of Australia's most qualified and brightest people. Although the Commission's current program of work is clearly impressive, many other Australian and overseas organisations could boast a similarly impressive work program. The distinguishing feature of the Commission is the set of principles that governs everything that it does.

The Commission continues a long and proud history of ensuring that all its work is governed by three core principles. Independence: The Commission operates under its own legislation, with an arm's length relationship to government. Transparency: The Commission's advice to Government and the information and analysis upon which it is based are open to public scrutiny. Its processes provide for extensive public input and feedback through public hearings, workshops and other consultative forums, and through the public release of draft reports and preliminary findings and its final report to Government. A community-wide focus: The Commission is required, by legislation, to take a broad view when conducting its work to ensure that its work encompasses the interests of the economy and the community rather than only the views of particular industries or groups.[7]

It's these three core principles that give the current work of the Commission its potency, its importance to the Australian Community and its international uniqueness. In practical terms, the strict application of these principles means that the government of the day can tell the Commission what it wants it to review, but not what to say in relation to those reviews.

The day-to-day application of these demanding principles has not been without cost to the Productivity Commission and its predecessors. Alf Rattigan describes how in 1973, the Country Party was '*completely opposed*' to the establishment of the Industries Assistance Commission.[8]

To successfully tread the very fine line of being both a creation of the government of the day, but having the responsibility to be independent of thought from that same government, the Chairs, leadership and staff of the Productivity Commission and its predecessors have been very careful in making public statements about the pressures that the Productivity commission and its predecessors have been under in the past when trying to tread this very fine line. However in 1998, Gary Banks, the new Chair of the Productivity Commission at the time alluded to this pressure. '*I am speaking to you today as the head of an organisation under some pressure. Still, it is hard to think of a time when it would not have been so. . . . Along the way previous commissions went through some difficult times, facing strong opposition from sections of industry and the union movement, as well as within government itself. The institution found itself under threat of closure or emasculation on several occasions*'.[9]

In addition to the published work of the Productivity Commission, it can be reasonably argued that the Commission and its predecessors have also contributed to the integrity of Australia's political and policy processes. Vested interests, seeking special benefits for themselves from governments, may be able to keep secret what they argue to Government behind closed doors. When dealing with the Productivity Commission, particularly during its open and transparent public enquiry processes into matters affecting them, these vested interests must expect to have their arguments and the benefits and costs of any government provided largesse to them subject to the 'sterilising' process of public disclosure and public analysis.

The media has been an essential part of ensuring that the work of the Productivity Commission and its predecessors is made public. Almost without exception, Commission reports are widely reported in the press. Headlines such as '*Labour market analysis is political dynamite*' or '*Report sets PM straight on health*' are common after the Commission releases one of its reports or its research. The views and opinions of the Productivity Commission and its predecessors have rarely been universally applauded in the press and the media, however in general, the press and the media have been consistent supporters of the open and transparent processes adopted by the Commission. The press and the media have also been the constant vehicle through which the Productivity Commission has conducted its conversation with the Australian people on critical matters affecting them.

Governments have often been frustrated and sometimes embarrassed by the independent recommendations or research of the Commission and its predecessors. Governments over the years have attempted to have it both ways. On the one hand, successive Governments, to their great credit have maintained the independence of the Commissions, while on the other hand have attempted to influence the direction and decisions of the Commission or its predecessors by for example, appointing a Chair, Commissioners, or Associate Commissioners who were thought to be sympathetic to the Government's ideological position.

Alf Rattigan, Chair of the Tariff Board and the inaugural Chair of the Industries Assistance Commission thought that he was probably appointed to these roles because he was 'saleable and manageable'.[10] History records however that Rattigan became synonymous with lower levels of protection for Australian industry and greater scrutiny of Government policies and became deeply respected by many leading politicians. Gough Whitlam as Prime Minister was able to say, in the face of criticism of the work of the Industries Assistance Commission 'I am a Rattigan man myself'.

Governments, frustrated by the independent and sometimes critical perspective by the Commission and its predecessors of government policy have even attempted to starve the Commission of government commissioned enquiries and reviews. John Button, the Industry Minister in the Hawke Labor Government, and for a period the Minister responsible for the Industries Assistance Commission described how this happens in practice.

'From time to time Carmichael (the Chair of the Commission at the time) complained that the commission didn't have enough to do. He suggested it might widen its scope and conduct an inquiry into the transport industry or the mining industry. In Cabinet the transport minister Peter Morris rejected an inquiry into 'his industry'. He liked a quiet life and was not keen on restructuring. Gareth Evans as Minister for Resources said the mining industry didn't want to be inquired into. So, nothing happened there either'.[11]

However, when governments have resorted to this form of control over the Commission, given the relative independence of the Commission and its predecessors, governments, to their frustration have had to simply watch on, as the Commission used its significant intellectual capability to produce its own independent research on topics that it regarded as important to the Australian community.

Sensible reform of the Commission and its predecessors has also come from politicians, who, while supporting the importance of the Commission or its predecessors, have identified the need for contemporising the focus and structure of these respective organisations. As Treasurer in the Keating Labor Government, John Dawkins was one such reformer. In the early 1990s, John Dawkins identified that as Australia was throwing of the efficiency-sapping yoke of tariff protection, more was needed to understand other significant impediments to the productivity of Australian organisations. As part of his personal reform agenda, Treasurer Dawkins decided to add 'Industry Development' references to the work of the Industry Commission. These new references caused significant discord within the Industry Commission at the time because of concern within the Industry Commission that this signaled a return, at least in part towards a desire by government for protection of Australian industry.

This concern was reinforced within the Industry Commission by the appointment of Bill Scales as the Commissions Chair. Scales had a long history in the Australian automotive industry, and prior to being appointed to the Industry Commission was the Chair of the Automotive Industry Authority, the body responsible for implementing the Hawke Labor Government's passenger motor vehicle reform program. It was suspected within the Industry Commission that this new form of reference combined with the appointment of Scales as Chair was aimed at reverting Australia to a past period of government financial support for specific industries, a concept that had been discredited by the Industry Commission, the Industries Assistance Commission and even the Tariff Board in the last years of its existence. However, both concerns proved to be completely without foundation. Like others before him, during his six years as Chair of the Industry Commission Scales ensured that the Industry Commission continued to contribute to the ongoing improvements of the efficiency of Australian industry in particular, and the Australian economy in general.

As it turned out, using these new forms of references from government, the Industry Commission was able to describe how, in a world of lower tariffs, Australia would need to address significant challenges to its overall competitiveness such as: poor transport infrastructure; excessive and restrictive regulation; gaps in Australia's international trading system and gaps in Australia's system of vocational education and training. These references made clear that reducing tariffs was a necessary, but not sufficient condition for improving the productivity of a particular sector of Australia's economy, nor sufficient for improving Australia's overall productivity performance.

However, this unsettling period of the history of the Commission and its predecessors does raise an interesting question. On the face of it, it seems that governments have seen the need to refocus these organisations around every decade without modifying the fundamental principle of independence, transparency and a community-wide focus. In retrospect, these re-foci have been beneficial for the organisation itself, and for the community at large. It has forced these recharged organisations to reconsider and reconceptualise the main sources of Australia's economic and social challenges and required them to find ways to address these challenges.

Other jurisdictions have subsequently adopted similar organisations. The New Zealand Government has established its own Productivity Commission, the Denmark Productivity Commission was established in 2012, the Norwegian Productivity Commission in 2014 and in 2015 the Chilean Government announced the establishment of its own Productivity Commission. And most telling, the Commission is also highly respected internationally with the OECD and the IMF often citing the Commission's work.[12] Closer to home, the South Australian, New South Wales and Queensland Governments have all established their own versions of the Commission. But not all governments have provided their particular Productivity Commissions with the legislated protection afforded Australia's Commissions. This makes these variations of the Commission more vulnerable to government influence and even abolition. The Victorian government abolished its Competition and Efficiency Commission in 2015.

Notwithstanding an ambivalence within governments about the risks of funding and providing a statutory organisation like the Productivity Commission with the independence it now enjoys, for almost 100 years, Australian governments of differing political persuasions have continued to do so. They have given these various organisations the funding and the authority to discuss critical matters of national importance with Australians in an independent and fully transparent manner and to do so with the interests of all Australians as its mission.

This is clearly worth celebrating. This is what makes the work of the Australian Productivity Commission unique.

Recognising poverty – the poverty line[13]

A fast and focussed way to address a problem is to measure it. In 1962, the newly created Director of the Institute for Applied Economic Research at University of Melbourne, Ronald Henderson, wanted to attract political and policy attention to ameliorate the plight of poor Australians. His interest had been stirred by a study, by the University of Cambridge, of acute poverty in southern Wales in the 1920s. This study revealed significant long-term damage to families from poverty and Henderson realised that the condition was probably also present in Australia.

To this end, in 1963, shortly after establishing his Institute, Henderson with the backing of his board, funding from the Myer Foundation and his own personal wealth, began a social welfare project. He brought together a multi-disciplinary group from economics (Dick Downing, John Harper), sociology (Jean Martin), statistics (Alison Harcourt) and social work (Margaret Harris) to 'do something' on the issue.

The team wanted to measure poverty, but how? Poverty is a fuzzy concept and the challenge was to find a metric that would be both acceptable and credible. The method Henderson's team chose was based on measuring the incidence of persons or families living below a reference minimum income. This measure, known as a poverty line, describes the amount of disposable income required to support the needs of different family configurations, given by the number of adults and children.[14]

The genesis of poverty lines came from the London School Board (see Gillie 1996) and was first implemented, separately, by Charles Booth and Benjamin Seebohm Rowntree in the UK at the turn of the 20th century.

However, in the halcyon days following World War II, it was widely believed that the new welfare state, together with the emergence of the affluent society, had finally put an end to poverty (Mendes 2008). This view began to be challenged from the late 1950s. In 1959, James Jupp wrote about the 'submerged tenth' of the Australian population including Aborigines, shack dwellers, deserted wives, unemployed migrants, slum dwellers and pensioners. Helen Hughes estimated that by 1960, about 330,000 widows, aged and invalid pensioners were living in poverty. Further research was also undertaken by the Victorian and Australian Councils of Social Service, the Brotherhood of St. Laurence, Ray Brown, David Scott, Leon Glezer, Michael Keating, John Stubb and John Nimmo (Mendes 2008).

Australians were therefore already becoming aware of the issue when the results from a larger-scale poverty survey (4,000 Melbourne households), undertaken by Henderson's group, were presented at an ANZAAS conference in 1967 by John Harper.[15] The results were dramatic and shocked the nation (Henderson, Harcourt and Harper 1970). An estimated 900,000 Australians were deemed to be living below the poverty line. This estimate did not go uncontested. In 1969, the Australian Minister for Social Security, Bill Wentworth, claimed that although the Government was committed to reducing absolute poverty, it could not be responsible for relative poverty which was the result of poor personal budgeting.

Strong voices emerged for a more systematic study of the extent and nature of poverty in Australia by the Anglican Church, the Australian Councils of Social Service and the Labor opposition (Mendes 2008). Under pressure, Liberal Prime Minister William McMahon agreed in 1972 to a Commission of Inquiry into Poverty with Ronald Henderson appointed as Chair. Later that year, the newly-elected Whitlam Labor Government extended the size and scope of the Inquiry, asking it to determine the extent of poverty in Australia, the groups most at risk of experiencing poverty, the income needs of those living in poverty, and issues relating to housing and welfare services. The outcome was a major report, *Poverty in Australia* (1975) which explored related topics such as law, education, mental illness, disability and consumer protection.

The Whitlam Government was social democratic by nature and committed to improvements in the standard and quality of life. In practice, this led to the introduction of universal health insurance, the abolition of university fees, significant increases to public pensions and benefits and legislation outlawing unequal pay based on gender. In principle, it also included comprehensive retirement incomes (superannuation) and a universal disability income insurance scheme, both of which were only implemented by later Labor Governments.

The subsequent Liberal Government, led by Malcolm Fraser, reiterated the need for Australia to maintain an income level below which a household should not fall. Fraser's emphasis was to provide security while encouraging initiative and self-reliance. Although he dismantled some of the welfare initiatives created by Whitlam, he accepted that widespread poverty exists, was substantial and needed to be moderated by public intervention. This legacy persists today.

In 1970, social security spending in Australia was about 7% of GDP. This rose to 16% under the Whitlam Labor Government but only fell slightly to 14% under the Fraser Government and is 19% today (2020). It is not possible to draw a definitive line from the Henderson Poverty Line to the rise of the welfare state in Australia, but given the prominence of Henderson's work on poverty, which is still well-known among the lay public today, it would be unreasonable to say it was a just a minor influence.

As shown elsewhere in this volume, Ronald Henderson has left a considerable mark on the Australian community. The secret sauce in his recipe for success in bringing important matters to public attention according to his colleagues was the loyalty and trust he engendered in his research team. He led with respect and made each member feel important contributors toward a visionary goal.

Since the 1975 Commission of Inquiry into Poverty, the Melbourne Institute has been publishing quarterly updates to the Henderson Poverty Line and it remains a valuable benchmark for poverty (Johnson 1987, 1996a; Wilkins 2007; Buddelmeyer and Verick, 2008).

Going metric

The conversion to metricisation, and its twin, decimalisation – both base-10 measurement systems – was relatively swift and painless in Australia. A staged approach was followed, and clear sunset dates were used beyond which imperial measures could not be quoted. This 'hard boundary' transition model contrasts with many other countries such as India, Hong Kong, the UK, the USA and Canada, which are still caught in a confusing imperial-metric limbo. Other countries which have completed conversion, such as the Republic of Ireland, took what might be described as the scenic route.

The metric system defines units based on the natural world (e.g. litres, grams, moles) with decimal ratios so that it is easy to arithmetically scale and convert units. Credit for the conception of the decimal numbering system lies with ancient Indian mathematicians. Subsequently, lone European scholars, Simon Stevin (1548–1620) and Gabriel Mouton (1618–1694), advocated and advanced the ideas of decimal fractions, decimal coinage, decimal weights and decimal measures. But it was the French Académie des sciences, in the 1790s, which first translated these ideas into action.

The first, and easiest, conversion is usually currency. Although ultimately the swap-over period in Australia was short, it was preceded by a long period of advocacy. Almost immediately after nation statehood in 1901, the first recommendation in Australia for a new decimal currency was made by a select committee of the House of Representatives (chaired by George Edward in 1902; Commonwealth of Australia, 1902). Subsequently, a Banking Royal Commission appointed by the Lyons Government made the same recommendation in 1937. Both these recommendations fell on deaf anglo-ears. It was not until after a 1960 Decimal Currency Committee report, chaired by Walter Scott, that a date – 14th of February 1966 – was set. Although Treasurer Harold Holt had set up the Committee, Prime Minister Menzies, a staunch monarchist, had been less than lukewarm. His compromise was to name the new currency a 'royal' but this proved so overwhelmingly unpopular that the Government quickly changed the name to a 'dollar' (Pfennigwerth 2016).

Public resistance to the changeover was limited and appeared swayed by the evidence. Much quoted research estimated that the one-off conversion cost of £30 million would be easily offset by an estimated £11 million ongoing annual saving – a considerable gain to business and household productivity (see Significant Achievements and the History of Measurement in Australia).

Arguably, the key to a seamless conversion was careful planning around public communication. Walter Scott made extensive use of radio, the press and direct marketing to households. There were extensive educational programs including animated cartoons; film and television appearances; comic strips; crosswords and puzzles; brochures and posters and editorial columns targeting minority sections of the community. Walter Scott made regular appearances on national television to reassure the community about the technicalities of the change.

People were given so much time to get used to the idea of decimalisation that every raised issue was addressed and ultimately it proved hard to argue against the merits. According to Rees (2016) '[t]here wasn't really any resistance. People took to it very quickly and there was a general air of optimism and positivity'.

The achievement of currency conversion opened the way for other forms of metrification. In 1968, a Select Committee of the Australian Senate, chaired by Keigh Laught, examined metric weights and measures and came to the unanimous conclusion that it was both practical and desirable to convert. There had been considerable preparatory work already. Australian schools had been teaching the metric system for some years and because of Australia's post-World War II immigration program about 10% of the population had used the metric system in their country of birth. According to Wilks (1992), it was decided not to use a referendum to rule on this change as relatively few people would have had sufficient knowledge of both systems to make an informed decision.

On 12 June 1970, the Australian Metric Conversion Act, passed by the Australian Parliament under Liberal Prime Minister John Gordon was given assent and by 1988 the last industry holdout – the real estate sector – converted to metric. In its deliberations, the Select Committee held 28 Public Hearings and 39 deliberative sessions; heard from 141 witnesses and accepted 54 written submissions. Almost all considered metricisation inevitable.

The task, however, was more daunting than currency conversion and required more detailed, technical education in specific industries. Consultative procedures were established through 160 committees, subcommittees and panels. Each industry was given the right and the responsibility to plan and implement conversion in its own way and to its own schedule. Individual companies were connected through their associations with their Sector Committee, and through them to the overarching Metric Conversion Board. Industry plans were drawn up and an army of foot soldiers were employed to personally visit businesses to explain the changes and what was expected of them. According to Chalupsky, Crawford and Carr (1974) and Wilks (1992), no industry was obliged to accept a program of conversion in which it did not have full say or which was devised by a body other than the industry Sector Committee or sub-committee.

There were many requests for help to understand the effects of these changes on people's daily lives and people were encouraged to only understand their needs in metric-speak – it was argued that there was no gain for translating to imperial in their heads. Information was widely provided to explain what a weather report in metric means in terms of warmth or sheep alerts or how much flour is required to feed the family. Because of careful planning, almost every road sign in Australia was converted within a month. To avoid consumer confusion, there were limited dual use periods and it became illegal to quote measures in imperial units beyond a set date. From 1974 for example, all new cars were fitted with metric-only speedometers. However, the imperial system continued to be taught for trade and general measurement purposes in schools and universities, so people could work with plans in both languages.

The role of international technical committees was influential. Mr AFA Harper, a research scientist, from CSIRO and technical consultant to the Senate Select Committee, was also Australia's representative on the International Organisation for Legal Metrology.

Conversion was not without its opponents. According to Goodyear (2013), there was an Australian Anti-Metric Association who were quite vocal in their opposition to metrication. However, their claims were so outrageous that they never gained traction with the public. In fact, the crafty Metric Conversion Board would invite representatives from the Association along with the press to their information sessions in order to get publicity for the conversion. So successful was the conversion of currency, weights and measures in Australia that its experience has been used as an exemplar by officials from the UK, Canada, the USA, Hong Kong, Singapore and Malaysia (Chalupsky, Crawford and Carr 1974; Wilks 1992).

So, what accounted for the smooth transitions in Australia compared with the UK and USA? According to Steele (2013) and the UK Metric Association, the key was the removal of dual systems by clearly defined implementation dates. Each industry and sector had to move towards metric, but they could do it in their own way and had responsibility for developing their own plan. Secondly, the Metric Board entertained no appeals for compensation which meant industry had to focus on getting the job done and not spend time rent-seeking. Both aspects stemmed from clear leadership with vision and plans by joined-up government sectors.

Universal health insurance – Medibank[16]

It took chutzpah and was a real cliff-hanger, but in 1975, Australia achieved a major win for access and equity in the form of universal health insurance.

Thanks to medical science, over the course of the 20th century, Australians had become progressively more confident that treatment by a doctor will leave you happier, healthier or both. As a corollary, the issue of access to this new wonder treatment – medicine – became a point of public debate.

Before the introduction of universal health care in Australia in 1975, health care was largely provided under a fee-for-service system, supported by voluntary private health insurance for those who could afford it and with charitable hospitals and doctors providing free services for pensioners. Since WWII, about 50% of the Australian population subscribed to voluntary health insurancew leaving an estimated 17% of households both uninsured and ineligible for free services. Between 1937 and 1953, there were four failed attempts to rectify this situation in the form of a universal health plan. These failures largely arose from resistance from the Friendly Societies (the private health insurers) and the doctors' associations (Scotton and MacDonald 1993). By 1943 however, about three in four people from the general population supported universal health care (Smith and Wearing 1987).

The voluntary medical insurance scheme worked well for doctors but not for patients. Most uninsured people were low-income and there were no concessions to people with chronic or severe problems. Voluntary insurance costs were tax deductible and favoured those on high incomes. The British Medical Association in Australia ensured that only pensioners on the maximum pension qualified for free care thereby forcing part-pensioners to take out voluntary insurance (which was more lucrative for the doctors and hospitals). Hospitals kept pushing for people to be treated as private patients in public hospitals and the means tests got tighter.[17] The funding model for health care was becoming increasingly out-of-line with medical science's potential to deliver benefits for Australians.

Against this backdrop, Professor Ronald Henderson, the newly appointed Director of the Melbourne Institute of Applied Economic Research at University of Melbourne (1962) had a strategy. He had become convinced by his new (1965) appointee, John Deeble, to launch a health economics research program. With Henderson, John Deeble and Dick Scotton negotiated with the Commonwealth Department of Health to get and analyse its unpublished data that related to the underlying health of Australians. They also sample surveyed 5,000 people from health funds. In what was unusual for the time, they used computers to handle large volumes of transactions. This process was assisted behind the scenes by the deputy leader of the Federal Parliamentary Labor Party, Gough Whitlam, whose advisor, John Menadue, would lodge 'Questions on Notice' in the Federal Parliament to get previously unavailable information for their research. The resulting research was then fed back to Labor MPs, such as Dr Moss Cass, who progressed the ideas (Menadue 1999).

Their aim was to design a health funding system to improve the health of all Australians and cross subsidise the sick and poor, while containing costs. Public insurance operates by pooling risks (both random and self-induced) while being underwritten by public funds.[18]

In 1968, Deeble and Scotton laid the foundations for their plan for universal health insurance in the *Australian Economic Review* by laying out how the maze of different funding sources depended on illness, war service, age, means and membership of voluntary insurance organisations. More people were drawn into the Labor policy net. John Menadue drew up lists of economists (Ted Wheelwright), urban planners, scientists and political scientists (Sol Encel) for help to drive the bold reform plan for Australia.

Although the issue of health funding had been brewing in Labor circles since at least 1962, its precedence accelerated in 1967 when Gough Whitlam took leadership of the Australian Labor party. In 1968, Dr Moss Cass linked Whitlam with Scotton and Deeble as well as with key public health figures, Prof Rod Andrew (Monash University), Dr Jim Lawson (Footscray Hospital) and Dr Allen Christophers (Victorian State Health Department). The catalyst for change was the publication of the Scotton and Deeble 1968 article and subsequent promotion of their ideas by Max Walsh in the *Australian Financial Review*. Profile and advertising for the Deeble-Scotton plan was also inadvertently provided by the level of the ire from the Australian Medical Association (AMA). Later in 1968, Whitlam gave a talk to the medical staff at the Royal Prince Alfred Hospital in Sydney, proposing a national health insurance scheme based on a copy of the Deeble and Scotton paper (Cass, Encel and O'Donnell 2017).

After the 1969 Federal Election, the reform plan was opposed by all Federal Labor Members of Parliament, including the five medical practitioners, as they opposed its fee-for-service design. However, Bill Hayden, the Labor Shadow Minister for Health and Gough Whitlam thought the reform plan was a very significant factor in Labor's favour and made it official policy for the 1972 general election.

There was strong resistance to the new health plan – mainly from the AMA, but also from the existing private health funds. Bureaucrats listened with polite interest but largely assumed that institutional constraints were unchangeable. They thought that people outside bureaucracies underestimated the difficulty of changing institutions. There were inquiries (e.g. Nimmo) and the continuation of public debate, but it was the carriage of the idea by Bill Hayden that was pivotal in turning an idea into political action. He visited the US, Sweden, Israel, UK and Canada; met with many opponents and engaged widely at public events and with the media.

Dick Scotton spent two years in Canada to learn more about their system – how to make data yield important insights, cost containment, operational efficiency, managerial control, computer systems and potential delays in claims processing. He discovered what sort of computer system was going to be needed to support the system and who would be the right Canadians to later hire (as the skills did not exist in Australia at the time) (Scotton and MacDonald 1993).

After the election of the Whitlam Labor Government in 1972, Hayden took charge of getting the health insurance program moving and appointed Scotton and Deeble as ministerial advisers. However, there is a large gulf between policy on paper and putting these programs into action. A key person in this translation was Ray Williams who saw the future in automated information processing (he had computerised the age pension); was a canny team builder and had an eye for talented people.

The argy-bargy between Hayden, the doctors' associations, the private insurers, hospitals, health bureaucrats and State Governments over the next three years can fill volumes, but needless to say, the sticking points were about money, profits and control and not what was in the best interests of the population.[19] Opponents of universal health plans were notable at the time for their increased used of professional political experts, market researchers, PR consultants, media advisors, advertising and lobbyists.

In 1974, following a double dissolution of Parliament, and the election of a second Whitlam government the six health bills were passed 95 to 92 in a joint sitting of Parliament. Medibank was launched on 1 July 1975. Over the following year there was a drop in private health insurance of 19% and an increase in public hospital patients by about 10%. The Fraser Government which won Government in late 1975 brought in a 2.5% levy on taxable incomes to pay for the scheme (with exemptions for low income earners). The desire by the Fraser government to dismantle universal health insurance was tempered by its popularity as throughout this period over 50% of people wanted no change to the original Medibank scheme (Scotton and MacDonald 1993). In 1983, the Hawke Labor government re-introduced the original 'Hayden plan', now renamed Medicare, with tighter financial controls.

Forward to 2020, and the debates continue. Medical academics are increasingly noting that fee-for-service is not the ideal mechanism for rewarding practitioners – GP or specialist – and those criticisms are increasingly being voiced by others. Some research finds that health care is superior where doctors are on salaries compared to fee-for-service practices.

Australian life expectancy is now second only to Japan despite having a relatively low portion of GDP spent on health services. It's worth reflecting on the route travelled in relation to this successful policy innovation. Given the changed Australian academic landscape with its focus on publishing in foreign journals about research matters with international appeal, neither Deeble nor Scotton would be likely to be hired now by a research organisation that has a focus on publication in foreign journals and because of the current focus on publishing research in foreign journals they certainly would not be encouraged to publish their research in an Australian journal.

Collecting financial support for children[20]

Policy intentions are just that unless followed through with efficient execution. And so, even though, by the mid-1980s, the Australian Government legally required non-custodial parents to pay for the support of their children, the actual number of parents complying was dismally low. Less than 30% of sole parents were receiving regular income support from non-custodian parents for the support of their children in Australia – a pattern the world over (McDonald 1985; Pirog and Ziol-Guest 2006; Garfinkel, Meyer and McLanahan 1998; Skinner, Bradshaw and Davidson 2007).

Prior to the mid-1980s, support for Australian children of separated parents was either agreed privately or determined by court order. Although courts typically struck very low rates of payment, orders were regularly flouted and custodial parents were often forced to rely on the slender payments from general government revenues or irregular support from families and friends. The result was extreme poverty for many of the children in these families and a poverty trap for many of the sole parents who faced work disincentives via the punitive income test for public benefits (Cass 1993; Hanasz 2017).

According to Edwards (2019), the problem at the time was easy to articulate: why should children suffer because their parents had decided to separate? Why should tax payers foot the bill? The solution was clear. What could possibly go wrong?

In 1984, Brian Howe became the Minister for Social Security under the new and reforming Hawke Labor Government. Although social security payments were about one-third of the Federal budget, the general opinion was that there was little that could be done to improve this behemoth portfolio. Howe had other ideas. He not only has had a canny knack for negotiation and getting things done but was widely acclaimed as an inspiring minister with a strong sense of what was right. Howe managed to sell the idea of using the tax office to collect payments from non-custodial parents to help pay for the support of their children to the relevant Cabinet sub-committee which included Prime Minister Hawke, Paul Keating, Treasurer; Peter Walsh, Minister for Finance; Lionel Bowen, Attorney-General; Susan Ryan, Minister Assisting the Prime Minister on the Status of Women and Don Grimes, Minister for Community Services.

The first thing Howe did was identify the priorities for his new portfolio. He used his connections at the Australian National University to organise a seminar of experts and reformers – Bettina Cass, Patrick Troy, Meredith Edwards, among others – to thrash out ideas (Cass 1988). They took a leaf out of Ronald Henderson's poverty inquiry, which had recommended that individuals should receive a guaranteed minimum income and decided to make a guaranteed minimum income for children their top priority.

Building an evidence base around the idea was next on the agenda. He appointed Bettina Cass to the social policy unit, within the Department, to lead a review of Australia's social security system. He knew that to get things done, he needed to actively spot experts who embraced a reforming zeal. Key people – Fiona Tito, Meredith Edwards, Deena Shiff and Lisa

Barker – were recruited to this review. This review produced a series of issues papers, one of which was concerned with the collection of payments for the support of their children from the non-custodian parent.

Collection was only part of the measures being considered – a more generous funding formula was central – but without efficient collection, formulae and court orders mean nothing. The new collection method, proposed and led by Edwards, was essentially a new-to-the-world and radical innovation. This method was to get the employer to deduct payments from workers' wages, along with normal income tax collections, before payment to the worker. The intention was that the child payment portion would then be collected by the tax office and transferred directly to the custodial parent. It was a system that was so simple and efficient that it was basically a 'no-brainer'. As strange as it sounds today it was opposed all along the social security chain of command. It was just considered an 'impossible reform'.

The original idea to use the tax office to collect payments from non-custodial parents came from Professor Irvine Garfinkel, an economist and social worker, at the Wisconsin Institute for Poverty. Garfinkel's mentor, Harold Watts, had previously suggested using annual tax returns to recoup payments from delinquent parents. Garfinkel improved this idea by suggesting that payments be withheld via the regular payroll system. Unfortunately, Wisconsin never had the opportunity to enact this idea, but Edwards had read his paper and pursued the idea. She and Shiff travelled to the USA to meet Garfinkel and later brought him to Australia to help build local support. This culminated in a road trip around Australia by Edwards and Shiff to build broader community backing for the reform.

Leading the opponents of this new collection system was the Department of Social Security hierarchy who had previously tried and failed to set up a collecting agency to achieve these same aims. At first, they did not take the review seriously, then they kept putting up different arguments for why it could not be done and finally they moved Edwards out of the building on the basis that she and her team posed a safety risk. Undeterred, a team of dogged and well-informed lawyers, Tom Brennan and Deena Shiff, met every point of active and passive resistance. The never took no for an answer and worked out solutions for each 'insurmountable' barrier.

The Australian Taxation Office was also strongly opposed to the idea. It wasn't their job; it would cost too much to run; it should be done by Centrelink; their systems were set up for batch processing not counter services; it would open the door for all manner of debt recovery. Ultimately, it took the intervention of the Treasurer, Paul Keating, who directed the Office in somewhat colourful language to just 'do it'.

Nonetheless, Edwards, Howe and their teams did find individual allies among the politicians. The Attorney-General, Gareth Evans, and the Minister for Health, Neal Blewett, were supportive. Importantly both the Prime Minister, Bob Hawke, and the leader of the opposition, John Howard, believed it was the right thing to do which gave the reform an unusual tail wind and an example of the importance and power of political bi-partisanship if it can be achieved.

Selected people in the bureaucracy also helped. Bill Burmester, from the Department of Finance assisted with modelling and undertook a forensic analysis of the additional costs that the Australian Taxation Office and Department of Social Security were claiming for the implementation. Everyone had their hand up for compensating revenue. Even the legal services wanted extra funding. Mary Finn from Attorney-General's Department and Mary Ann McLachlan from the Office of the Status of Women were supporters and helped develop a package via an interdepartmental committee. However, the Attorney-General's department was initially sceptical as it did not want to surrender any part of their responsibility for the family court to an administrative body.

According to Howe, ministers who want reform ultimately realised that they must persuade departments to change. It was a matter of finding the touch points for each minister or department, such as improve circumstances for the disadvantaged; achieve financial savings; ensure equitable treatment for the children of single income families; reduce the burden on the courts; or just improve general efficiency.

Unlike many other innovations, there were few peak community groups behind this reform. The Lone Fathers' Association ran an advertising campaign against the scheme; the Single Mother and Her Child, and ACOSS, the main national welfare advocacy body, were ambivalent and worried about forcing mothers to name the father. Shiff's experience, from her days at the Australian Law Reform Commission, meant that she knew the importance of engaging early and often with opponents.

A more positive role was played by many journalists, such as Kate Legge from *The Age*, and her contribution was influential in getting the general population on side (Edwards 2001). Not all journalists, however, viewed the changes in a positive light. In 1987, David Clarke (*Australian Financial Review*) reiterated the views of the Lone Fathers' Association and the Law Council that the scheme would have 'unintended consequences' and should not proceed.

It did not go unnoticed that almost all decision makers in the Department of Social Security, Cabinet, the press gallery and related agencies, were men, and more than a few were non-custodial fathers. These were the times when the number of women in Parliament could be counted on one hand and halls of power were dominated by a tight male culture. Child support became a gender issue with some people depicting it as a feminist plot against men.

Ultimately, given that most opposition was about how the algorithm for payments would be drawn, Howe split the change into two stages: a more readily acceptable new collection system for payments first with the more contentious algorithm later.

The Child Support (Registration and Collection) Act was passed in the Federal Parliament in 1988 and this established the Child Support Registrar within the Australian Taxation Office. The Registrar maintains a register of maintenance liabilities and garnishes the wages or salaries of liable parents to be passed to custodial parents via the Department of Social Security. As expected, the administrative costs were found to be low with experts rating Australia as the most cost-effective system along with New Zealand, Norway and Sweden. In New Zealand and Australia, the administrative cost has been estimated as 12–14% per dollar collected compared with 23% in the USA and 17% in Wisconsin (Skinner, Bradshaw and Davidson 2007).

The innovation does not just stop with establishment. The ability of the Child Support Registrar, located within a somewhat hostile Australian Taxation Office, needed continual backing to ensure that it was staffed by willing and able people and was not neutered through passive neglect. That non-compliance with child support orders has disappeared as a notable social problem is a credit to this organisation.

Like innovations in science and technology, social innovations also build on prior innovations. The antecedents of Irvine Garfinkel's idea was Watts's proposal for collecting child support through annual tax returns combined with the knowledge that US income tax had transitioned in its early days from annual to weekly pay-as-you-go employer deductions. The descendent of this idea was the income-contingent student loan scheme (conversation with Bruce Chapman).

As of 2021, few other countries have used employer deductions from earnings as the main method of collection from non-custodial parent to help pay for the support of their children, relying instead on deductions from bank accounts or pensions (Skinner, Bradshaw and Davidson 2007). New Zealand adopted an employer deduction scheme on 1 November 2021 and is managed by their Inland Revenue department.

Income-contingent student loans – HECS[21]

As a driver of economic growth, economists have long since mulled over the when and wherefore of the accumulation of machinery and infrastructure (Smith 1776; Marshall 1890; and followers). But the importance of intangible capital – skills, capabilities, systems, know-how and just ideas more generally – had tended to fall under the radar. If these intangibles are a more significant source of wealth than machines, then our best minds have been looking in the wrong place.

And so, it may be. There is now an emerging consensus that intangible capital contributes at least equally to economic wealth than tangibles such as plant, equipment and infrastructure (e.g. Roth and Thum 2013; Crass and Peters 2014; Roth, Sen and Rammer 2021; Bontempi and Mairesse 2015). Marshall (1920) sowed the seeds for this theory but evidence only started to emerge after World War II.

Friedman and Kuznets (1945) was an early study to formally estimate the return on human capital – that is, higher education. They found that the return was substantially greater than for physical capital (see also Walsh 1935). It made them wonder – why don't people invest more in education and less in machines? It must be, they surmised, because the capital market imperfections arising from the risks to borrowers and lenders of unsecured loans limited people's ability to borrow to invest in education. Perhaps, they surmised, if individuals could sell rights over their future income to finance investment in their own education, this anomaly would be corrected.[22] This idea of loan repayments based on future earnings became known as income-contingent student loans (Barr 2016; Reischauer 1989).

From the 1960s, income-contingent student loans were actively discussed by economists, at least within the Anglophone world. They were seriously considered in a 1963 review to overhaul of the higher education system in the UK, but ultimately were not recommended (UK Robbins Report 1963).[23] The matter, however, that put a loans scheme into serious contention was not an abstract concern with market failure, but the pressure caused by growing numbers of professions requiring university education, twinned with the financial dependence of most universities on government funding – a burning platform.

As this problem was common to all developed countries, the debates continued. Arguments in favour of these loan schemes were concentrated at the London School of Economics (Mervyn King, Nicholas Barr, John Barnes and Iain Crawford); around the USA (Robert Reischauer, William Simpson, Wayne Riddle); in Australia (Bruce Chapman); as well as New Zealand (Gary Hawke).[24] The trick was to design a scheme that would contribute to the rising costs of higher education, encourage the interested and able to enter university, but not penalise people who earned low post-graduate incomes. According to Chapman (2005), all countries recognised that free higher education was unsustainable as governments were simply not prepared to increase taxes or reduce public services to support it. However, up-front student fees were regressive and inequitable, and, regardless of the political persuasion of the government-of-the-day, would violate societal standards of fairness.[25]

A 1970s incarnation of a loan scheme at Yale University led by James Tobin failed because it pooled repayments for the whole class of students and thereby discouraged ambitious people from enrolling in the scheme. But this error was quickly diagnosed and did not dissuade analysts from proposing alternative funding options (Nerlove 1975; Chapman 2005).

But the question is really, given that many countries were on the precipice of taking action; the debate had matured; and the need was great: why was Australia the first country to successfully launch a student income-contingent loan scheme? The likelihood of introducing this loan scheme in Australia was not high as the incumbent party in government – the Labor Party – was philosophically opposed at the time to user-pays mechanisms.

Key senior members of the new Hawke Labor Government, elected in 1983, understood that 'free' merely meant someone else was paying. John Dawkins, as Minister for Finance in the first incoming Hawke Labor government had spent several years as shadow minister for education and accepted the experts' evidence that free higher education meant a transfer of income from the average tax payer to the (soon-to-be) wealthy graduate. Together with fellow Perth colleague Peter Walsh, Minister for Finance who replaced Dawkins as Finance Minister in 1984, he was determined to ensure that the person who has most to gain from higher education, paid for it, or at the very least, paid for the private benefit they received from their higher education.

John Dawkins had staffed his office with people who knew the tertiary education system well. Peter Noonan, with a background in student unionism and higher education had overall responsibility for the tertiary education sector in Dawkins private office and was very familiar with and sympathetic to the general ideas implicit in the concept of student income-contingent loan schemes. David Phillips, a secondee from the Federal Department of Education was also an influential staff member in Dawkins private office and was one of the co-drafters, with Bruce Chapman, of the Terms of reference of the highly influential Wran Committee report. This report recommended the eventual basic structure of Australia's student income-contingent loan scheme.

In 1987, Dawkins hired economist Bruce Chapman from the Australian National University as a consultant to help to make it happen by producing a report that outlined the benefits and costs of a 'user pays' system for higher education in Australia.

There were two keys to the ultimate success of the introduction of Australia's approach to a student income-contingent loan scheme (Chapman 2014). The first was designing a system that did not induce the wrong type of behaviour (as exhibited in the Yale experiment) or put undue stress on low-income earners post-graduation. The second was finding a cost-effective system for collecting loan repayments once a student was earning an income.

Chapman and colleague Meredith Edwards realised that piggy-backing on facilities for employers to withdraw taxes and charges from wages on behalf of the tax office was the most efficient solution. Simple in theory but not in practice. Organisations like tax offices typically do not like taking on additional responsibilities, especially involving something new and therefore risky. The key struggle was then getting the tax office to agree that it would be suited to the role.

There followed Chapman's issues paper and a green paper report (from the separate Wran committee) and these both met with the anticipated resistance. Although the initial level of the loans provided to students to cover their tuition fees was very modest (amounting on average to about 20% of tuition costs), the broader Labor party opposed its user-pays mechanism and the National Students Union opposed it outright. The student rallies were violent and persistent and scarcely veiled death threats were made – against Chapman in particular. According to Higgins (2019) the complexity and novelty of the policy made it hard to explain to the public and there were many misunderstandings. However, with persistence from John Dawkins, especially in facing down the Labor party's left-wing, understanding emerged and attitudes changed, and the public eventually acknowledged that deferred contingent repayments would not harm access (Chapman and Nicholls 2013; Chapman 2015).

Words matter and describing the scheme as 'free at point of entry', rather than 'free', allayed many fears within the Labor party. Having the backing of influential people was also critical. Dawkins had the confidence of Prime Minister Bob Hawke, Treasurer Paul Keating and Australian Council of Trade Unions President Simon Crean.

However, the Labor Government did not control the Senate (the upper house) and support was needed from one other party for the Bill to pass. Ultimately, the Australian Democrats came on-board after it was made explicit the magnitude of the additional funds each university would miss out on if the scheme was not implemented (the Liberal party led by John Howard opposed the Bill). Needless to say, lobbying pressure from universities in favour of the scheme was pivotal in getting support from the Australian Democrats.

The Bill passed, and the income-contingent student loans scheme swung into action and it became the demonstrator of success around the world (Larocque 2009). It was followed by a similar scheme in New Zealand in 1993 and by 2020, it has been implemented, with local variations, in about a dozen other countries.

The scheme is not static (Barr et al 2019). There have been several revisions to the scheme, including varying the loan level by discipline (in part to re-align with a new changing education fee structure), and extending it to the cost-of-living, post-graduate studies and vocational training.

As a mechanism to underwrite community risk, income-contingent loans have considerable welfare implications. Israel has a tradition of advancing sales-contingent loans to businesses wanting to undertake innovations and Chapman has argued for the concept to be considered for drought relief, arts and sport bursaries, legal aid and extended parental leave. Whatever one thinks about the theoretical arguments for the student scheme, it has been a key ingredient in allowing the Commonwealth Government to extend university education from about 7% of school completers in the 1980s to 40% today. A success by any measure.

Comprehensive retirement income – compulsory superannuation

Australia is not unique in having a comprehensive policy approach to retirement income. However, it is amongst the few countries in the world to have what the World Bank has described as the preferred approach to retirement income policies, that is government policies that support a retirement income system consisting of 'a publicly managed system with mandatory participation . . .; a privately managed, mandatory savings system; and voluntary savings' (World Bank 1994, p. xiv).

A central recommendation of the 1994 World Bank Report was the application of what the World Bank described as a multi pillar system where there were multiple financing sources that could share responsibility of old age support (World Bank 1994, p. 10).

The intention here is not to describe all elements of Australia's retirement income system and the public policies that support it. Others have done that more than adequately. The intention here is to show how the second pillar of Australia's retirement income system, what the World Bank described as 'a privately managed, mandatory savings system' (World Bank 1994, p. xiv) came about.

This is important for two reasons. Once established, significant public policies such as a nation's retirement income system are hard to change, and yet Australia has been able to introduce significant changes to this important area of public policy. Second, this second pillar became law in 1991, some 82 years after the introduction of the first pillar in Australia's system of retirement income – Australia's aged pension scheme. Australia's experience in the reform of its retirement income system, therefore, can give encouragement to other nations wishing to implement difficult reforms of its own retirement income system, even when the fundamentals of such systems are entrenched within a nation's political psyche and may seem impervious to change.

However, it would be a mistake to think that Australia's system of retirement income was deliberately designed with some grand view of an ideal approach to supporting people in retirement. Each element of Australia's comprehensive retirement income policy emerged independently to address issues thought to be important at the time, and it is only in hindsight that Australia's retirement income system can now be seen in total as being consistent with the World Bank's view of best practice retirement income policy.

Nor should it be assumed that Australia's retirement income policy is settled. This is far from the case with both marginal and significant variations to the details of all elements of government policy in this area a feature of Australian politics and public policy.

From early in Australia's post-colonial history, Australia has had elements of what the World Bank observes as a multi-pillar retirement income system. The elements of these early retirement income systems were not universally applied across the Australian continent and even where they were applied they were not integrated within a coherent retirement income system. In the early 1900s, the States of New South Wales and Victoria established their own means-tested pension schemes, which was relatively quickly followed by Queensland in 1908. In 1908, the newly established Commonwealth government created the Invalid and Old Age Pensions Act 1908. At that time this newly minted aged care-pension was 'limited according to character, race, age residency and means' (Nielson and Harris 2010, p. 2). The original purpose of the Australian aged pension was designed only to provide a modest social welfare net for the elderly (Warren 2008, p. 2).

Occupational superannuation schemes however are much older. For example, the Bank of New South Wales, Australia's first bank, established in 1817, also created Australia's first occupational superannuation scheme in 1862. Until the early 1990s, occupational superannuation mainly applied to Commonwealth and State public servants, members of the defence forces and a select few white-collar employees in companies in the private sector. Warren argues that by 1974, 32.2% of Australia's wage and salary earners had some form of occupational superannuation (Warren 2008, p. 11).

The third element of Australia's retirement income policy, that is, voluntary savings and investments was ostensibly a matter for individuals to determine. However, because Australia's aged care pension was from its inception, and still is means tested, the level of private assets, savings and investments affects the extent to which an individual is eligible to receive an aged pension, and the amount an individual is eligible to receive.

This basic framework for Australia's retirement income policy remained until the mid-1980s. Until the mid-1980s, Australia's retirement incomes policy consisted of an Aged Pension, which was designed as a minimum income safety net for the elderly, superannuation for a select group of around one third of Australia's workforce, and voluntary, private savings or investments. However, on both sides of Australian politics, there had been for some time an interest in the possibility of significantly extending the scope of occupational superannuation as a more important element of Australia's system of retirement income. This is where Australia's experience gets interesting.

The story of the introduction of a comprehensive industrial based occupational superannuation scheme is most often discussed within the context of the Australian Labor Governments of Bob Hawke and Paul Keating (Bramston 2016, p. 257), (Edwards 1996, p. 419, p. 440), (Kelly 1992a, p. 201, p. 206), (Kelly 2009b, pp. 144–147), (O'Brien 2015, pp. 159–160).

However, like the development and implementation of most successful public policies, the truth about the origins of Australia's approach to compulsory occupational superannuation is a little more complicated.

From the mid-1960s, both sides of the Australian political spectrum showed interest in the introduction of this last leg of Australia's retirement income system. In 1972, in the dying days of the McMahon coalition government, Prime Minister McMahon announced its intention to conduct a committee of enquiry into national retirement benefits which included the possibility of establishing a national superannuation scheme (McMahon 1972). This committee of enquiry led by Sir Leslie Melville, an eminent Australian economist and public servant, focussed on how to best to create a means-test-free pension for people aged 65 and over. The possibility of establishing a national superannuation scheme was regarded as a means of financing this initiative. This initiative of the conservative Australian Coalition government was cut short with the defeat of the McMahon Government.

This interest continued with the election in 1972 of the Whitlam Labor Government. Gough Whitlam[26] announced that if elected the Australian Labor Party would establish a national superannuation scheme (Whitlam 1977, p. 279). The Whitlam Labor government made good on its promise and in 1973 established a National Superannuation Committee of Inquiry led by Professor Keith Hancock, a distinguished economist and labour-market historian from Flinders University to advise on how such a scheme might be established. However, again, politics intervened. By the time the Hancock Committee had completed its work, the Whitlam Labor government had been replaced in 1975 by the Liberal-Country party Fraser Government. The Fraser government did not proceed with the implementation of any of the recommendations of the Handcock Committee but the seeds of reform had been sown (Warren 2008, pp. 11–12).

Although changes to Australia's approach to occupational superannuation remained off the Fraser Government's agenda, superannuation schemes were beginning to gain popularity within unions, especially the unions within the building and construction industry (Mees 2017, p. 244). These industry-based occupational superannuation schemes were to eventually develop their own particular form of management structure with the funds under management self-administered initially by unions and eventually by a joint industry union-employer governance structure (Mees 2017, pp. 245–247). What then followed was further industry-based superannuation schemes in other industrial sectors of the Australian industrial workforce supported and facilitated by the Australian Council of Trade Unions, and in particular, its secretary, Bill Kelty and its assistant secretary, Gary Weaven. These schemes tended to follow the governance structure first established by the initial building industry schemes.

Although both sides of the Australian political spectrum had tinkered with the idea of implementing a national, compulsory occupational superannuation system it wasn't until the election of the Hawke Labor government that the ideas that formed the basis of Australia's universal and compulsory occupational superannuation system went beyond just ideas and good intentions and were implemented. But even then, the road to enactment was not smooth. It would be wrong to see the initial establishment of compulsory occupational superannuation in Australia as part of some grand vision to establish a model retirement incomes policy. In fact, Australia's superannuation scheme was born out of economic necessity.

In August of 1985, Treasurer Paul Keating brought down the Hawke Labor government third national budget. The background included a warning from Australia's central bank, the Reserve Bank, that Australia faced significant economic head-winds: 'include the large current account deficit, emerging signs of a wages drift, the sluggish performance of the manufacturing sector and evidence of rising overall pressures on capital markets' (Bramston 2016, p. 256). In response to the pressure on wages, Paul Keating used this budget to dampen wage demands by the unions by introducing what was described as Accord Mark II, which offered the union movement a 2% tax cut and the introduction of a 3% compulsory occupational superannuation in return for reduced wage demands and improvements in productivity (Bramston 2016, p. 257). This was a master stroke by Treasurer Keating and ACTU secretary Bill Kelty. It provided the government of the day with a mechanism for keeping wages and employment conditions in line with productivity growth. It also provided the union movement with a long-held ambition to ensure that all the Australian workforce had access to compulsory occupational superannuation, and importantly, it set in train the establishment of the last supporting pillar of what is now Australia's comprehensive retirement income policy.

Australia's compulsory occupational superannuation policy has undergone many changes since its inception in the mid-1980s. Over time, it has grown to become an important plank of Australia's savings and investment effort. From its modest beginnings, compulsory occupational superannuation contributions have increased from 3% of a worker's ordinary time earnings in 1986 to 10% in 2021. The Australian Prudential Regulation Authority, the financial system prudential regulator, reported that in June 2021, Australian superannuation assets totalled around AUD$3.3 trillion (APRA 2021) and is now larger than the total assets held on the Australian Stock Exchange.

As Australia's system of compulsory occupational superannuation has matured it is now a portable benefit between employers. Workers can also select their own manager of their superannuation assets. Australian

governments have also increased the level of transparency and accountability of superannuation funds by the annual publication of the investment
performance of these funds under management and increasing the ability of
fund members to change to funds with better financial performance.

Australia has come a long way in ensuring that all Australians have the
opportunity to live comfortably in retirement. Australia's retirement income
system is not perfect, and no doubt will undergo significant changes as, like
many other nations, its population ages. However, whatever is to come next
in its evolution, Australia's system is better prepared today than it was up
until the 1980s because of the recent development of Australia's compulsory
occupational superannuation system.

Privatisating state enterprises

Of all of Australia's recent economic reforms, the privatisation of public
assets by the Commonwealth, State and Territories, and Local governments
in the 1990s would have to be amongst the most controversial.

In the 1990s, Australian governments, national and state, were one of
the world's most aggressive appliers of the practice of privatisation of public assets. Between 1990 and 1997, Australia was second only among the
OECD nations to the United Kingdom in terms of the absolute value of privatisations, and second to New Zealand relative to Gross Domestic Product.
The Reserve Bank of Australia estimated that between 1990 and 1997, the
value of privatisations by Australian governments was around $61 billion,
with the Commonwealth and the States involved in equal measure. During
this time, the Commonwealth was involved in the privatisation of financial
services and communications and the States were involved in electricity, gas
and transport (Reserve Bank of Australia 1997, p. 8).

During the 1990s, it was mainly the Commonwealth and the Victorian
governments that became involved in the significant privatisation of public
assets. From 1990 until 1997, the Commonwealth privatised, or part privatised the Commonwealth Bank, some airports, Telstra, Australia's largest
telecommunications provider and Qantas, Australia's national airline for
around $27.8 billion. In addition, the Victorian Government privatised elec-
tricity assets for around $22.5 billion. Several State insurance businesses
were privatised for around $3.1 billion and the State Banks in New South
Wales, Western Australia and South Australia were privatised for a total of
around $2.2 billion (Reserve Bank of Australia 1997).

However the pattern of privatisations has not been consistent across Australian jurisdictions either during the 1990s, or during the first two decades
of the 21st century. Infrastructure Partnerships Australia records details
of the number and the value of privatisations by year and by jurisdictions

(Infrastructure Partnerships Australia, July 2020). Although the Commonwealth and Victoria were the main users of privatisation in the 1990s, the number of privatisations declined significantly during the 2000s. However Victoria increased its privatisation activities significantly from 2014. South Australia had a smaller number of privatisations. New South Wales was also involved in privatising public assets during the 1990s, but not to the same extent as Victoria. However, since the year 2000, privatisation increased significantly in New South Wales and has been dominated in terms of value by the privatisation of energy and port assets totalling around $48bn.

Western Australia was active in privatising public assets during the latter part of the 1990s but has not proceeded with any significant privatisations so far during the 21st century. Tasmania was relatively inactive in relation to privatisation both during the 1990s and during the first part of the 21st century with only a small number of privatisations. Queensland had a small number of privatisations by number and value during the 1990s, increased the number by value and number between 2007 and 2014, and has had no significant privatisations since that time. Both the Australian Capital Territory and the Northern Territory were not involved in privatising public assets during the 1990s or the first decade of the 21st century and were involved in only a very small number of privatisations by number and value from 2015 (Montoya and Ismay 2017).

However, discussing privatisations, just in terms of the raw number of public assets sold and their sale value, masks the intensity of the debate that often surrounded these privatisations. The more recent contemporary approach to privatisations in Australia had a somewhat unusual beginning. It all began with a dispute about the marketing of eggs. The deregulation of the production and marketing of eggs in New South Wales, and the sale of the assets of the New South Wales Egg Corporation in 1989 was small in value but created significant tension and acrimony amongst the egg producers of New South Wales. The decision by the leaders of the New South Wales Egg Corporation to seek their privatisation created such acrimony within the New South Wales egg industry, that it became a harbinger for the resistance that could be expected from those individuals or groups who considered themselves to be disadvantaged by privatisation. The *Australian Financial Review*[27] described the debate as a 'civil war' between interstate egg producers (Stutchbury, 1991). All States and Territories learned from this relatively obscure example of reform by the New South Wales Greiner Coalition Government. It was also an early and very salutary lesson for those involved in the privatisation process about the need to clearly articulate the community-wide benefits of privatisation, to consult widely about its likely effect on key stakeholders, and to be well prepared for the inevitable backlash from those who may see themselves as disadvantaged by reform.

Similarly, governments learned from the very significant privatisations in Victoria during the 1990s. A key lesson to come from the Victorian privatisation experiences was the importance of detailed preparation, extensive communication with the community about the expected benefits and strong, determined leadership. When in opposition, Liberal Member of Parliament, Alan Stockdale, prepared well for a privatisation agenda based on lessons from previous privatisations in New South Wales, New Zealand and Thatcher's British Government. When the Kennett Coalition government came to power in Victoria in 1992, not only did Stockdale as Treasurer in the Kennett government provide the intellectual drive and leadership of the significant privatisations in Victoria during this time, importantly, he also instituted significant innovations within the privatisation process that benefited subsequent Australian governments with their privatisation efforts. Interestingly, whereas New Zealand was very active in privatising public assets during the 1990s, it privatised only a very small number of public assets after that time, contrary to the Australian experience (Cardo and Wilson, 2012).

Stockdale took prime responsibility for the detailed implementation of Victoria's privatisation activities out of the hands of the Victorian bureaucracy and placed it in the hands of external experts, skilled in asset sales. Stockdale said 'We took it (the privatisation process) out of the hands of bureaucrats' and 'in effect privatised the process' (Fearon 2002, p. 41). Stockdale established the 'Electricity Supply Industry Reform Unit' to design and implement the privatisation of Victoria's electricity assets. This unit was, by design, led by an outsider, Peter Troughton, a former British telecommunications engineer, with a successful history of difficult corporate restructuring. Troughton, who was not only tough, he was not only an outsider to the Victorian public sector, but also an outsider to Australia (Parkinson 2000, p. 187).

Importantly, assets were restructured prior to privatisation. The Victorian Government structurally separated the generation, transmission, wholesale and retail elements of the State Electricity Commission prior to privatisation. In addition, it then went further and structurally separated parts of the generation and retail elements of the Victorian electricity network. The Government also put in place regulation, albeit what might be best described as light-handed regulation, of the 'monopoly' elements of the system – the transmission and distribution elements of the system (Fearon 2002, p. 41).

This not only provided the opportunity for the government to obtain the very best sale price for these very valuable public assets, it gave the best chance to stimulate competition in the generation and retail section of the electricity market, post privatisation. Stockdale also used the same general principles and process for the successful privatisation of Victoria's gas assets in the late 1990s.

All Australian governments learned from the Victorian experience, in the same way that Victoria and other Australian governments learned from international experience and in particular, the New South Wales Government's deregulation and privitisation of egg production and marketing. This form of national 'learning by observing' by Australia's national, State and Territory governments, through the process of 'cooperative, competitive federalism' has served Australia well in relation to privatisations and other reforms since the early 1990s.

Privatisation in Australia remains controversial. Privatisation goes back to the post World War II Liberal Menzies government. The Commonwealth Oil Refineries was bought by BP; the Government enterprise Comalco was bought by Rio Tinto Alcan; the Australian Aluminium Production Commission became The Bell Bay aluminium smelter (Harris 2002, p. 35). During late 1980s and throughout the 1990s, surveys of the Australian people consistently showed a clear preference for holding services, such as Telstra, Australia Post, the Commonwealth Bank, Qantas and railways, in public hands (Kelly and Sikora 2002, p. 54). Kelly and Sikora argued that the community saw none of the subtlety about different reasons for privatisation such as the effect on resolving a government's fiscal challenges or improving the performance of a state-owned entity. People tended to see all privatisation in the same light.

The definition of what constitutes privatisation was, and to some extent, is still hotly contested within Australia. The Reserve Bank of Australia defines privatisation as: 'the full or partial transfer of ownership of public assets to the private sector. This process refers to the sale of enterprises which are a "going concern" rather than the sale of land or buildings' (Reserve Bank of Australia December 1997). However, others take a much broader view of what constitutes privatisation in the Australian context. Aulich and O'Flynn describe privatisation as including: 'divestment of public enterprises, outsourcing of the delivery of public services and increases in the cost recovery by government agencies' (Aulich and O'Flynn 2007). In more recent times, the privatisation of public assets has been increasingly referred to by governments as asset or capital recycling, to indicate the intention by governments to use the proceeds of the sale or long-term lease of a public asset to fund the establishment of other contemporary and needed public assets or services.

Whatever the definitional scope, Australia has been at the forefront of privatisation over the past 30 years and privatisation has been a very significant tool in the public policy toolbox of the Commonwealth and State governments. In addition, whether narrowly or broadly defined, the motivation for privatisation by governments has varied and consists of ideological, necessity, efficiency and pragmatic reasons. The Thatcher Conservative Party government was one of the first governments to embark on a wholesale process of privatisation of public assets. By Thatcher's own admission, these privatisations were for broadly ideological purposes.[28]

The privatisations of the Victorian Kennett government during the 1990s, like almost all other Australian privatisations, had multiple objectives but the overriding urgency was the need to reduce the Victorian Government's debt. Parkinson argues that in fact, the State of Victoria was in danger at that time of the unprecedented risk of defaulting on its debts (Parkinson 2000, p. 144).

There was also a strong desire, however, within this newly minted Kennett Coalition Government to improve the overall productivity performance of Victoria's State-Owned Enterprises. This could have been achieved by other means such as changing the leadership and management of these organisations or creating a more corporatised governance structure, but the rate of improvement would likely to have been incremental.

The Commonwealth Governments of Hawke, Keating and Howard during this same period were more pragmatic in their motivations and intentions. The Hawke Labor Government during the 1980s although ambivalent about privatisation eventually came to embrace privatisation as part of its broader micro-economic reform agenda. Megalogenis argues that the privatisation motive of the Keating Labor government was to 'remove government from businesses it had no reason to be in, such as banking and air travel' (Megalogenis 2008, p. 201).

Of course, policy initiatives such as privatisation do not develop in a vacuum. During the 1990s, Australian governments were not alone in the use of privatisation to achieve certain public policy goals. During the period of the late 1970s and throughout the 1980s, international bodies, as well as Australian governments and organisations were watching and learning from international experience about the privatisation of public assets, particularly what was happening in Thatcher's Great Britain. Parker argues the Thatcher government actually had no defined overall privatisation plan, and the policy of privatisation evolved with the success of each privatisation transaction (Parker 2004). The World Bank found that during the 1980s and early 1990s, around 6,800 state-owned enterprises were privatised, with over 2,000 of these in developing countries (Kikeri, Nellis and Shirley 1992, p. 2).

In Australia, organisations such as the Centre of Policy Studies, at Monash University, and subsequently, the Tasman Institute, both sometimes described at the time as free market think tanks, and led by Professor Michael G Porter, were arguing that to improve Australia's economic performance, Australia should follow the example set by the Thatcher government. Other organisations, such as the Industry Commission, were also bringing to the attention of the community the potential benefits from wide-ranging micro-economic reform, including reforms of government-owned businesses (Industry Commission 1990).

As discussed previously, Alan Stockdale, the treasurer in the Kennett Government, had studied the privatisation experiences of other countries when in opposition. Similarly, the Keating Labor Government commissioned a report on National Competition Policy, the 'Hilmer Review', to help further stimulate Australia's micro-economic reform effort. This report had the effect of changing the face of Australian governments and would eventually have a profound impact on the operation and ownership of the public assets of all Australian governments (National Competition Policy 1993).

The 'Hilmer Review 1993' led by Professor Fred Hilmer (University of New South Wales) was commissioned by the Keating Government, with the agreement of the leaders of all Australian States and Territories to recommend an Australian approach to competition policy and laws. The Panel recommended strengthening institutions regulating competition across Australia and creating the Australian Competition and Consumer Commission and the Australian Competition Council. However, the real power of the Hilmer Review was the power of the arguments put by the Panel in relation to the benefits to Australia from a competitively neutral environment for all Australian businesses, public or private. In essence, the Hilmer Review powerfully exposed the costs to the State and the community from the lack of reforms of these State-owned businesses.

Treating all organisations the same, and creating competitive pressures on all organisations equally, public or private, created opportunity for the demonisation of the idea, and of those promoting it. Megalogenis describes the majority public view at that time. 'Competition policy would become a dirty word throughout the second half of the 1990s for the wrong reasons' (Megalogenis 2008, p. 51). Competition Policy was portrayed by those threatened by competition as pitting everybody against each other. The fact was that it was aimed at a relatively small group within society, and in particular, organisations such as monopoly public utilities, and professions that were at the time protected from competition by specially designed regulatory arrangements. That the removal of any special privilege would be subject to a form of 'public interest test', didn't seem to assuage public concern. Competition policy did not of itself promote privatisation, but it did make the ownership of public utilities in particular less attractive to governments due to the increased risk of their decline or failure in the face of intense competition.

Privatisation has been a very significant element of Australia's micro-economic focus for the past 30 years. During the 1990s, Australia was one of the world leaders in privatising public assets, both in terms of the value of assets privatised and in terms of their contributuon to gross domestic product and the increase in Australia's overall increase in its productivity performance. The motivations of government to privatise public assets and the means by which privatisation has been applied has varied, and governments have continued to privatise public assets in the face of public scepticism, and often, public hostility. Australia's privatisation efforts have not been even across the past 30 years but have, however, continued when Australian governments have found it appropriate, and the opportunities have been favourable to do so. There have been many vocal and many thoughtful critics of privatisation, and some reasonably doubt as to whether the benefits touted by governments from some specific privatisations have been achieved. However, there is no doubt that the privatisation activities of Australian governments, for all their benefits and costs have been at the forefront of international privatisation activities and have been an important plank of Australia's economic reform efforts.

Managing a river basin – best practice or work-in-progress?[29]

For many Australians, one of the over-riding images of the past 20 years is of the devastating effects of Australia's Millennium drought on the environment in the Murray-Darling Basin. This drought began in about 1996 and continued until 2010. Regarded as the most severe drought in Australia since white settlement, the Millennium Drought affected most of Southern Australia. It caused the closing of the great Murray River to the Indian Ocean at the Coorong and the Lower Lakes, the geographical end point of the Basin, and also seriously affected the health of around 70% of the iconic Australian River Gums along its 20 major river systems (Bond, Lake and Arthington 2008, p. 4).

In addition, in the summer of 2018 and 2019, Australians were confronted with disturbing pictures on their television screens of millions of dead fish including the iconic Murray Cod, lying 'belly-up' in the Darling River at Menindee, a small town of around 550 people 110 kilometres south-east of Broken Hill. These were devastating images. Sara Tomevska, the local Australian Broadcasting Corporation journalist said: 'It was just as far as you could see big grey Murray Cod floating to the surface. It was apocalyptic, almost. . . . It was surreal' (Simons 2020, p. 37).

These highly visual and practical examples of a disturbing environmental calamity caught the immediate attention at the time of not only the Australian public, but also of Australian politicians. The locals saw it as a failure of the ongoing management of the Basin; the politicians blamed it on the drought.

Managing river basins in a contemporary context is difficult, particularly when they traverse separate countries, or separate jurisdictions within the one country. Managing river basins inevitably demands taking into account the diverse needs of many stakeholders including farmers, irrigators, the water needs of communities within those river basins and importantly, the ongoing environmental health of the basin itself. Many continents have river basins so in that regard Australia is not exceptional. In a world where second-best resource management is the reality, Australia may be exceptional in the way it has attempted to manage the Basin. However, any success that Australia has had in managing the Murray-Darling Basin was a long time coming.

The Murray-Darling Basin covers around one million square kilometres that is, one seventh of the land mass of Australia and dominates much of the landscape of south eastern Australia (Blomquist, Haisman, Dinar and Bhat 2005). It supports around 9,200 irrigated agricultural businesses with an annual turnover in agricultural products of AUD$24 billion and a tourism industry worth A$8 billion. It is also environmentally important, not only to Australia but internationally, being home to an identified 120 waterbirds and over 50 native fish species and with 16 internationally recognised protected wetlands. Importantly, the Murray-Darling Basin is home to more than 40 Aboriginal nations (Murray-Darling Basin Authority Annual Report 2020–21, p. 8).

If the Murray-Darling Basin were a horse, it would be described as a wild horse that simply will not be tamed. During the past 130 years the Basin has seen devastating floods in 1909, 1917, 1921, 1931, 1950, 1952, 1956, 1974, 1993, and 2021 and heart-breaking droughts in 1895, 1914, 1944, 1968, 1981, 1997 and 2013 (Murray-Darling Basin Authority 2020). The level of rainfall within the Basin is never the same from year to year. It completely refuses predictability.

The first settlers began exploring the Basin in the 1820s and as the use of the river system increased, there was a greater need to come to an arrangement between the various stakeholders within the Basin to share water. In 1914, the Commonwealth, New South Wales, Victoria and South Australian governments signed the River Murray Waters Agreement. This agreement set out the need and the means to develop infrastructure (locks, dams and weirs) in the southern Basin, and to store and share water between the three states. Australia's attempts to manage the competing demands for water use by the various stakeholders has evolved in three distinct and overlapping phases and has been driven by three very distinct historical necessities.

Phase one of Australia's attempt to 'control' the Basin was determined by Australia's Federal constitutional structure, put in place at the time of Australian Federation in 1901. At Federation, the States of Australia were provided with constitutional responsibility for all water resources within their state boundaries. This constitutional responsibility was enhanced in 1914 with the establishment of the River Murray Waters Agreement. This agreement attempted to codify the rules between the riparian States of New South Wales, Victoria and South Australia for the sharing of water within the River Murray system. In 1917, the States further formalised this arrangement with the establishment of the River Murray Commission to administer the River Murray Water Agreement. These governance and administrative arrangements continued until the late 1980s and is best described as a 'State Based' system of governance and management with underpinnings from intergovernmental agreements, but little role for the Commonwealth Government.

From 1901 until the 1980s, the main activity of these arrangements was the construction and operation of water storage infrastructure such as dams, weirs, locks and barrages that primarily benefited the three riparian States and subsequently leading Horne to claim that 'Australia has the highest per capita water storage capacity of any country' (Horne 2016, p. 28).

In 1981 the mouth of the River Murray first closed, an indication that the river was dying due to a combination of increased use and a drying climate. Not only was there increasing and unsustainable demand for water, but serious environmental challenges were beginning to emerge. In 1980–1981, the salinity levels in the Basin were amongst the highest ever recorded and in 1987, mouth of the river Murray again closed because of insufficient water flows.

In 1987, in response to these challenges, the riparian states replaced the River Murray Waters Agreement with the Murray-Darling Basin Agreement, which was intended to expand the sharing of water resources within the State boundaries of the riparian States to cover the whole of the Basin. It also expanded the scope of the agreement to include the health of the landscape as well as the health of the river system within the Basin. The governance of the Basin was enhanced with the establishment of a Ministerial Council that is made up of government ministers from each of the jurisdictions covering the Murray-Darling Basin and the Commonwealth of Australia, and a Community Advisory Committee.

This period of reform of the arrangements for the efficient allocation of water coincided with Australia's significant microeconomic reform initiatives such as the reduction of historically high import tariffs; the deregulation of the financial system and corporatisation of public enterprises.

Phase two of the contemporary management of the Basin began formally in 1988 with the establishment of the Murray-Basin Commission to attempt to better coordinate the activities between the States and Commonwealth governments. These reforms were stimulated by the eventual, albeit grudging acknowledgement that the riparian States acting alone would not be able to address these challenges. During this phase, the States also began to experiment for the first time with the use of contemporary pricing tools for the allocation of water.

In 1994, the Council of Australian Governments (COAG) agreed in principle to separate statutory surface water rights from land rights. However, this unbundling of rights was to be a long, convoluted process (Horne 2016, p. 30). The new agreement also brought environmental health as well as other externalities such as salinity explicitly into consideration. Importantly, increased funding from all governments and increased community scrutiny was added with the addition of a Community Advisory Committee. According to Blomquist, Haisman, Dinar and Bhat, the success of the COAG reforms was due to better intergovernmental cooperation, instituting mechanisms for stakeholder participation and the provision of trusted data about basin problems (Blomquist, Haisman, Dinar and Bhat 2005, p. 28).

Depending on your perspective, Phase three of the contemporary management of the Basin came about *because* of the Millennium Drought, or *to take advantage* of this crisis. According to Bell (forthcoming), the Millennium

Drought exacerbated distributional tensions over water allocations amidst mounting awareness of special dealing, rent seeking and privileged interests. The legitimacy and trust in State governments to manage the Basin had been undermined (Bell forthcoming). Whatever the motivation, the reforms in this phase in the evolution of the governance and management of the Basin were significant. Phase Three officially began in 2007 with the introduction into the Australian Parliament of the Water Act 2007, and the replacement of the Murray Basin Commission with the Murray-Darling Basin Authority. This signalled a step-change in the collective, holistic and sustainable management of the Basin on behalf of Australian people.

It is hard to fully capture the ferociousness of the ongoing debate in Australia, lasting more than 130 years, about the nature of the allocation of water across the Basin. Heated town hall meetings have rallied farmers, fishers, residents, Wentworth Group of Concerned Scientists and peak bodies such as the Victorian Farmers Federation, the Growers' Wine Group, Australian Conservation Foundation and Environment Victoria. Since the Millennium Drought, this debate has primarily focused on the competing water demands of commercial irrigators, large and small, the critical human water needs of those living within the Basin, the demands of the environment and more recently, the cultural needs of Australia's first people. By reconciling these competing claims, the various decision-making bodies 'crab-walked' towards finding a solution to managing one of Australia's most scarce resources, water.

While progress in managing the often conflicting demands of the various stakeholders within the Basin often seems to be interminably slow, Horne and Grafton have argued that during this latest period of the contemporary management of the Basin the basic and fundamental preparatory work, conducted by scientists, at the request of the Murray-Darling Basin Ministerial Council and the Murray Darling Basin Commission, underlay any ownership by stakeholders to the 'solutions' to the effective management of the Basin. They argue that changes were made in the long-term interests of the Basin and its various stakeholders and were not just transitory political make-overs (Horne and Grafton 2019, p. 172).

The 2007 Millennium Drought reforms introduced a role for the Australian Consumer and Competition Commission,[30] a more prominent role in environmental water management and the provision of $3 billion to purchase water entitlements for environmental purposes. In addition, complementary Commonwealth Government programs focused on the future prospects of the irrigation sector and irrigation district efficiency and the provision of enhanced water information (Horne and Grafton 2019, p. 176). It prompted urgent and lasting initiatives such as the establishment of the Living Murray program – a program aimed to recover 500 gigalitres of water for the environment.[31]

In the context of the historical governance and management of the Basin, these were radical reforms. According to Horne and Grafton, these changes occurred because the Liberal Prime Minister John Howard and water minister at the time, Malcolm Turnbull, were prepared to act and take responsibility for the difficulties thrown up by the Millennium Drought (Horne and Grafton 2019, p. 181). Turnbull credits whatever successful changes that were implimented at that time to the combination of political determination, outstanding policy advice and a focus on the realities of the lived experience of those affected by political decisions. He called it one of the successful domestic policy initiatives of the Howard Coalition Government.[32]

It would be naïve to argue that all is perfect with the governance and management of the Basin or that the optimal allocation of water, for the two million people that call the Basin home, has been achieved. It is clear that notwithstanding the challenges, Australia has acknowledged these challenges and is not naïve about how difficult they are to surmount. The most important lesson that Australia brings to the international debate about the management of river basins is the need to be realistic about the challenges of governing and managing river basins; to continuously focus on the development of policy tools that will assist in their management, and importantly, no matter how long it takes, to be ready to take the difficult political and public policy actions to resolve the competing demands when the opportunity to do so presents itself.

The World Bank has called the Murray-Darling (Basin) Commission, the predecessor to the current Murray-Darling Basin Authority, the 'paragon of modern-day river basin management' (Mody 2004, p. 9). These international experts have placed Australia as leaders in river management because they understand the immense political and policy difficulties standing in the way of governing and managing river basins. Australia is clearly imperfect in the management of the Murray-Darling Basin, but nonetheless is at the frontier of an important journey.

Notes

1 Sincere thanks to Gary Banks for his very helpful and insightful comments.
2 Productivity Commission (2017–2018).
3 The Economist (2018).
4 Rattigan (1986, p. 3).
5 Rattigan (1986, p. 21).
6 Minister for Trade (Mr J McEwen) (1968).
7 PC News – May 2019.
8 Rattigan (1986, p. 188).
9 Productivity Commission (2003, p. 2).
10 Rattigan (1986, p. 9).
11 Button (1998, pp. 264–265).
12 Productivity Commission Annual Report (2017–18).
13 Our grateful thanks to Alison Harcourt and David Johnson for information and comments.

14 A detailed description of the calculation and use of poverty lines is published in the *Australian Economic Review*, 4th Quarter 1987 and a discussion of their limitations is published in the *Australian Economic Review*, 1st Quarter 1996.

15 The research staff was expanded to include Sheila Shaver, Jean McCaughey, Helen Ferber and Roger Layton (Williams 2012).

16 Grateful thanks to Ross Williams and Moss Cass.

17 Scotton and MacDonald (1993) claim that in the spirit of the Menzies era, it was private but not competitive.

18 They said that '[t]he crucial fact of health care financing is that social objectives require a much greater pooling than [voluntary] insurance alone can provide'. (p 11). Adverse selection meant that under voluntary insurance, only the sick will insure with the result that insurance schemes needed government subsidisation to function.

19 Deeble (2009) recalls 'I remember . . . the cloak and dagger meetings with the optometrists over an agreement to bulk bill and the frigid contacts with ophthalmologists. But it happened. The optometrists signed up, the medical benefit payments stopped, and the ophthalmologists immediately ceased to do any eye refractions at all, without any of the disastrous income effects that they had predicted'.

20 Grateful thanks to Brian Howe, Meredith Edwards, Irv Garfinkel, Fiona Tito Wheatland, Tom Brennan and Deena Shiff.

21 Thanks to Bruce Chapman, John Dawkins and Peter Noonan.

22 There are several variants of income-contingency loan models. In this early version repayments continued over each year of the individual's working life regardless of the amount of the original loan.

23 Contributors Peacock and Wiseman (1962), Prest (1962) and Blaug (1966) were in favour of an income-contingent student loan scheme.

24 Although these groups were not necessarily in contact with each other. Chapman, who was not an education economist, in particular, was not aware of these northern hemisphere debates at the time.

25 Except for the US where fees were and remain the norm.

26 The leader of the Australian Labor Party, in his Party's Policy Speech before the December 1972 Australian national elections.

27 *Australian Financial Review*, February 1, 1991.

28 'Privatisation . . . was fundamental to improving Britain's economic performance. But for me it was also far more than that: it was one of the central means of reversing the corrosive and corrupting effects of socialism. . . . Just as nationalism was at the heart of the collectivist program by which Labour Governments sought to remould British society, so privatisation is at the centre of any program of reclaiming territory for freedom' (Thatcher 1993, p. 676, quoted in Parker 2004, p. 3).

29 Grateful thanks are due to James Horne for comments on this draft.

30 Australian Competition and Consumer Commission.

31 This was at six icon sites: the Barmah – Millewa Forest in NSW; the Gunbower – Koondrook – Perricoota Forests in Victoria; the Hattah Lakes in Victoria; the Chowilla Floodplane and the Lindsay – Wallpolla – Mulcra Islands that cover part of both Victoria and South Australia; the Lower Lakes, Coorong and Murray River Mouth in South Australia and the River Murray Chanell in South Australia.

32 As a sign of the political importance of these national reforms, Malcolm Turnbull, who was to become Australia's 29th Prime Minister regarded these reforms as being so important as to have devoted six pages of his autobiography to his role in their design and implementation (Turnbull 2020, pp. 131–136).

References

Aulich, C. and O'Flynn, J., 2007. From Public to Private: The Australian Experience of Privatisation. *The Asian Journal of Public Administration*, 29(2), pp. 153–171.

Australian Prudential Regulation Authority, 2021. *APRA Releases Superannuation Statistics for June 2021*, www.apra.govoay/news-and-publications/apra-release-superannuation-statistics-for-june-2021.

Barr, N., 2016. Milton Friedman and the Finance of Higher Education. In *Milton Friedman: Contributions to Economics and Public Policy*, edited by Robert A. Cord and J. Daniel Hammond, Oxford University Press, New York and Oxford, Ch. 23, pp. 436–463.

Barr, N., Chapman, B., Dearden, L. and Dynarskid, S., 2019. The US College Loans System: Lessons from Australia and England. *Economics of Education Review*, 71, pp. 32–48.

Bell, S., forthcoming. *The Limits of State Capacity in Australia's Murray-Darling River Basin*

Blaug, M., 1966. Loans for Students. *New Society*, 8(210), pp. 538–540.

Blomquist, W., Haisman, B., Dinar, A. and Bhat, A., 2005. *Institutional and Policy Analysis of River Basin Management: The Murray Darling River Basin, Australia*, World Bank Policy Research Working Paper 3527, February 2005, Wold Bank Washington, DC.

Bond, N., Lake, P. and Arthington, A., 2008. The Impacts of Drought on Freshwater Ecosystems: An Australian Perspective. *Hydrobiologia*, 600, pp. 3–16.

Bontempi, M.E. and Mairesse, J., 2015. Intangible Capital and Productivity at the Firm Level: A Panel Data Assessment. *Economics of Innovation and New Technology*, 24(1–2), pp. 22–51.

Bramston, T., 2016. *Paul Keating: The Big Picture Leader*, Scribe, Melbourne, Australia.

Buddelmeyer, H. and Verick, S., 2008. The Dynamics and Persistence of Income Poverty in Australia. *Economic Record*, 84(266), pp. 310–321 (An earlier version appeared as IZA Discussion Paper No. 2827).

Burrell, S. and Stutchbury, M., 1994. *Australia Rebuilds: The Recovery We Had to Have*, The Financial Review Library, Melbourne, Victoria.

Button, John, 1998. *As It Happened*, Text Publishing, Melbourne.

Cardo, A. and Wilson, W.R., 2012. *Privatisation: The New Zealand Experiment of the 1980s: How DID Mom and Pop Fare?* https://ssrn.com/abstract=2178696.

Cass, Bettina, 1988. *Income Support for the Unemployed in Australia: Towards a More Active System*, Issues Paper (Social Security Review (Australia)) No. 4, Australian Government Publishing Service, Canberra.

Cass, B., 1993. Sole Parent Family Policy in Australia: Income Support and Labour Market Issues. *Social Policy Journal of New Zealand*, 1, pp. 3–16.

Cass, M., Encel, V. and O'Donnell, A., 2017. *Moss Cass and the Greening of the Australian Labor Party*, Australian Scholarly Publishing, North Melbourne.

Chalupsky, Albert B., Crawford, Jack J. and Carr, Edwin M., 1974. *Going Metric: An Analysis of Experiences in Five Nations and Their Implications for U.S. Educational Planning*. Final Report. American Institutes for Research in the Behavioral Sciences, Palo Alto, Calif. National Inst. of Education (DREW), Washington, DC.

Chapman, B., 2005. *Income Contingent Loans for Higher Education: International Reform*, The Australian National University, Centre for Economic Policy Research, Discussion Paper No. 491, June 2005 Canberra.

Chapman, B., 2014. Interview with Jan Libich Chapman B. *Education Financing: Government as Risk Manager?* Melbourne: La Trobe University.

Chapman, B., 2015. Obstacles on the Way to Reform. In *So You Want to Be a Leader: Influential People Reveal How to Succeed in Public Life*, edited by Philip Crisp, Hybrid Publishers, Melbourne, Australia, pp. 202–214.

Chapman, B. and Nicholls, J., 2013. *Higher Education Contribution Scheme (HECS)*, Canberra: Crawford School Asia and the Pacific Policy Studies Research Paper, 2.

Commonwealth of Australia, 1902. *Report from the Select Committee on Coinage*. Commonwealth of Australia, 3 April 1902, Melbourne, http___www.aphref.aph.gov.au_house_committee_reports_1902_1902_ppd4.pdf.

Crass, D. and Peters, B., 2014. Intangible assets and firm-level productivity. *ZEW-Centre for European Economic Research Discussion Paper*, Mannheim, (14–120).

Deeble, J., 2009. *Le plus ça Change: Recollections of a Retiring Health Economist*. The Chalmers Oration 2009, Flinders University Medical School, Dr John Deeble AO Emeritus Fellow, Canberra: The Australian National University.

The Economist, 2018. Aussie Rules: What the World Can Learn from Australia, 25 October 2018.

Edwards, J., 1996. *Keating: The Inside Story*, Viking Penguin, New York.

Edwards, M., 2019. The Child Support Scheme: What Innovative Collaboration Can Achieve. In *Successful Public Policy: Lessons from Australia and New Zealand*, edited by Joannah Luetjens, Michael Mintrom and Paul Hart, Canberra: ANU Press Series: Australia and New Zealand School of Government (ANZSOG), pp. 139–164.

Edwards, M., Howard, C. and Miller, R., 2001. From Child Maintenance to Child Support: An Unlikely Policy Reform. In *Social Policy, Public Policy: From Problem to Practice*, edited by M. Edwards, Allen & Unwin, Sydney.

Fearon, P., 2002. From Stockdale to Stocktake: Privatisation and Deregulation of the Victorian Electricity Industry. In *Privatisation: A Review of the Australian Experience*, edited by M. Mead and G. Withers, Melbourne: Committee for Economic Development of Australia.

Friedman, M. and Kuznets, S., 1945. *Income from Independent Professional*, National Bureau of Economic Research, New York, p. 352.

Garfinkel, I., Meyer, D.R. and McLanahan, S.S., 1998. A Brief History of Child Support. In *Fathers Under Fire: The Revolution in Child Support Enforcement*, edited by I. Garfinkel, S.S. McLanahan, D.R. Meyer and J.A. Seltzer, New York: Russell Sage Foundation.

Gillie, Alan, 1996. The Origin of the Poverty Line. *Economic History Review*, 49(4), pp. 715–730.

Goodyear, Peter, 2013. *More Than a Mile Behind: America and the Metric System*, https://milebehind.wordpress.com/2013/07/21/an-australians-take-on-metric-system-adoption/, accessed 16 July 2020.

Hanasz, P., 2017. History of the Child Support Scheme. In *The Social Sciences Shape the Nation*, Canberra: Academy of the Social Sciences in Australia.

Harris, T., 2002. Accountability in Privatisation and Contracting Out. In *Privatisation: A Review of the Australian Experience*, edited by M. Mead and G. Withers, Melbourne: Committee for Economic Development of Australia.

Hawke, R., 2010. *The Inaugural Bishop Manning Lecture*, Sydney.

Henderson, R.F., 1975. *Poverty in Australia: First Main Report, April 1975*, Commission of Inquiry into Poverty, AGPS, Canberra.

Henderson, R.F., Harcourt, A. and Harper, R.J.A., 1970. *People in Poverty: A Melbourne Survey*, Cheshire, Melbourne.

Higgins, T., 2019. The Higher Education Contribution Scheme: Keeping Tertiary Education Affordable and Accessible. In *Successful Public Policy: Lessons from Australia and New Zealand*, edited by Joannah Luetjens, Michael Mintrom and Paul 't Hart, ANU Library Press, Canberra.

Horne, J., 2016. Water Policy Responses to Drought in the MDB, Australia. *Water Policy*, 18(S2), pp. 28–51.

Horne, J. and Grafton, R.Q., 2019. The Australian Water Markets Story: Incremental Transformation. In *Successful Public Policy: Lessons from Australia and New Zealand*, edited by J. Luetjens, M. Mintrom and P. Hart, Canberra: Australian National University Press, pp. 165–190.

Industry Commission, 1990. *Annual Report 1889–90*, Australian Government Publishing Service, Canberra.

Infrastructure Partnerships Australia, Privatisations by Year, https://intrastructure. org.au/chart-group-privatisations-asset-sales-by-year/, accessed 19 July 2020.

Johnson, D., 1987. The Calculation and Use of Poverty Lines in Australia. *Australian Economic Review*, 4th quarter, pp. 45–55.

Johnson, D., 1996a. For the Student: Poverty Lines and the Measurement of Poverty. *Australian Economic Review*, 1st quarter, pp. 110–126.

Johnson, D., 1996b. *Poverty, Inequality and Social Welfare in Australia*, Heidelberg, Germany: Physica-Verlag.

Kelly, J. and Sikora, J., 2002. Australian Public Opinion on Privatisation, 1986–2002. In *Privatisation: A Review of the Australian Experience*, edited by M. Mead and G. Withers, Melbourne: Committee for Economic Development of Australia.

Kelly, P., 1992a. *The End of Certainty: The Story of the 1890s*, Allen and Unwin, St Leonards, NSW, Australia.

Kelly, P., 1992b. *The End of Certainty: The Story of the 1980s*, Allen and Unwin, St Leonards, NSW, Australia.

Kelly, P., 2009. *The March of Patriots: The Struggle for Modern Australia*, Melbourne University Press, Carlton, Victoria, Australia.

Kikeri, S., Nellis, J. and Shirley, M., 1992. *Privatisation: The Lessons of Experience, The International Bank for Reconstruction and Development*, The World Bank, Washington, DC.

Larocque, N., 2009. *1 Tertiary Education Financing in New Zealand*. Student Loan Schemes: Experiences of New Zealand, Australia, India, and Thailand and Way Forward for Malaysia, p. 1. Kuala Lumpur: Penerbit Universiti Sains Malaysia.

McDonald, P.F. and Australian Institute of Family Studies (AIFS), 1985. *Economic Consequences of Marriage Breakdown in Australia: A Summary Compiled*, Melbourne: Institute of Family Studies.

McMahon, W., 1972. *National Retirement Benefits*, House of Representatives, Canberra.

Mees, B., 2017. Organisational Mimesis and the Emergence of Industry Superannuation in Australia. *Journal of Management History*, 23(3), pp. 241–258.

Megalogenis, G., 2008. *The Longest Decade*, 2nd ed., Scribe Publications, Carlton North, Victoria.

Menadue, John, 1999. *Things You Learn Along the Way*, Ringwood, Victoria: David Lovell Publishing, p. 63.

Mendes, P., 2008. *Australia's Welfare Wars: The Players, the Politics and the Ideologies*, Kensington NSW: University of New South Wales Press. ISBN 978-0-86840-991-7.

Minister for Trade (Mr J McEwen) Hansard, *House of Representatives*, 28 November 1968- and Referenced in a Lecture Delivered by Professor Richard Snape to the Economic Society of Australia, Victorian branch on 19 March 1997.

Mody, J., 2004. *Achieving Accountability Through Decentralization: Lessons for Integrated River Basin Management*, World Bank Policy Research Working Paper 3346, June 2004, http://econ.worldbank.org.

Montoya, M. and Ismay, L., 2017. *Privatisation in NSW: A Timeline and Key Sources*, NSW Parliamentary Research Services, Number 2/June 2017, https//www.parliament.nsw.gov.au.

Murray-Darling Basin Authority, 2020. *History of Water Management in the Basin*, August 2020, https//www.mdba.gov.au.

Murray-Darling Basin Authority, 2021. *Annual Report, 2021*, Commonwealth of Australia, https.//www.mdba.gov.au.

National Competition Policy, 1993. *Report by the Independent Committee of Inquiry, 1993*, Australian Government Publishing Service, Canberra.

Nerlove, M., 1975. Some Problems in the Use of Income-contingent Loans for the Finance of Higher Education. *Journal of Political Economy*, 83(1), pp. 157–183.

Nielson, L. and Harris, B., 2010. *Chronology of Superannuation and Retirement Income in Australia*, Parliamentary Library of Australia, Parliament of Australia, Canberra, ACT.

O'Brien, K., 2015. *Keating*, Allen & Unwin, Crows Nest, NSW, Australia.

Parker, D., 2004. *The UK's Privatisation Experiment: The Passage of Time Permits Sober Assessment*, CESIFO Working Paper No 1126, Category 9: Industrial Organisation, Blackwell Publishing, Oxford.

Parkinson, T., 2000. *Jeff – The Rise and Fall of a Political Phenomenon*, Penguin Books Australia Ltd, Ringwood, Victoria, Australia.

PC News – May 2019, www.pc.gov.au.

Peacock, A. and Wiseman, J., 1962. The Economics of Higher Education. In *Higher Education: Evidence – Part Two: Documentary Evidence*, Cmnd 2154-XII, HMSO, London, 1963, pp. 129–138.

Pfennigwerth, S. 2016. *The Introduction of Decimal Currency: How We Avoided Nostrils and Learned to Love the Bill*, Museum of Australian Democracy. www.moadoph.gov.au/blog/the-introduction-of-decimal-currency-how-we-avoided-nostrils-and-learned-to-love-the-bill/#, accessed 16 July 2020.

Pirog, M.A. and Ziol-Guest, K.M., 2006. Child Support Enforcement: Programs and Policies, Impacts and Questions. *Journal of Policy Analysis and Management*, 25(4), pp. 943–990.

Prest, A.R., 1962. The Finance of University Education in Great Britain. *Higher Education: Evidence – Part Two: Documentary Evidence*, Cmnd 2154-XII, HMSO, London, 1963, pp. 139–152.

Productivity Commission, 2003, www.pc.gov.au.

Productivity Commission. *Annual Report 2017–18*, www.pc.gov.au.

Rattigan, G.A., 1986. *Industry Assistance: The Inside Story*, Melbourne University Press, Melbourne.

Rees, Peter, 2016. *Inside the Vault: The History and Art of Australian Coinage*, Randwick NSW: New South Publishing, Royal Australian Mint Staff.

Reischauer, R.D., 1989. HELP: A Student Loan Program for the Twenty-first Century. In *Radical Reform or Incremental Change*, New York: College Entrance Examination Board, pp. 33–56.

Reserve Bank of Australia, 1997. *Privatisation in Australia*, Reserve Bank of Australia Bulletin, December 1997, www.rba.gov.au.

Robbins, L., 1963. The Robbins Report on Higher Education. *Report of UK Government Committee on Higher Education*, 22(1), pp. 43–49.

Roth, F., Sen, A. and Rammer, C., 2021. *Intangible Capital and Firm-Level Productivity – Evidence from Germany* (No. 9), Hamburg: University of Hamburg, Hamburg Discussion Papers in International Economics.

Roth, F. and Thum, A.E., 2013. Intangible Capital and Labor Productivity Growth: Panel Evidence for the EU from 1998–2005. *Review of Income and Wealth*, 59(3), pp. 486–508.

Scotton, R.B. and Macdonald, C.R., 1993. *The Making of Medibank*, Australian Studies in Health Service Administration No 76. Randwick NSW: School of Health Services Management, University of New South Wales.

Significant Achievements and the History of Measurement in Australia. Department of Industry, Tourism and Resources – National Measurement Institute. https://www.industrysearch.com.au/history-of-measurement-in-australia/f/363. Archived from the original on 30 September 2009, accessed 9 June 2006.

Simons, M., 2020. *Cry Me a River: The Tragedy of the Murray-Darling Basin*, Quarterly Essay, Issue 77, 2020, Schwartz Books Pty Ltd, Carlton, Victoria.

Skinner, C., Bradshaw, J. and Davidson, J., 2007. *Child Support Policy: An International Perspective* (No. 405), Corporate Document Services, Leeds.

Smith, R. and Wearing, M., 1987. Do Australians Want the Welfare State? *Australian Journal of Political Science*, 22, pp. 55–65.

Steele, John, 2013. *Comment on Metrication in Australia*, http://metricviews.org.uk/2013/06/metrication-in-australia/#comment-32705, accessed 16 July 2020.

Stutchbury, M., 1991. NSW Cracks Egg Boards' Protective Shell. *Australian Financial Review*, 1 February, www.afr.com/politics/nsw-cracks-egg-boards-protective-shell-19910201-k4a19.

Turnbull, M., 2020. *A Bigger Picture*, Hardie Grant Books, (Melbourne) Richmond, Victoria.

UK Metric Association, https://ukma.org.uk/press/comparison-with-australia/, accessed 16 July 2020.

Walsh, J.J., 1935. *Education of the Founding Fathers of the Republic*, Books for Libraries, Freeport.

Warren, D., 2008. *Australia's Retirement Income System: Historical Development and Effects of Recent Reforms*, Melbourne Institute Working Paper Series: Working Paper No 23/08, Melbourne Institute of Applied Economic and Social Research, The University of Melbourne, Victoria, Australia.

Whitlam, E.G., 1977. *On Australia's Constitution*, Widescope International Publishers Pty Ltd, Camberwell, Victoria.

Wilkins, R., 2007. The Changing Socio-Demographic Composition of Poverty in Australia: 1982 to 2004. *Australian Journal of Social Issues*, 42(4), pp. 481–501 (An earlier version appeared as Melbourne Institute Working Paper No. 12/2007).

Wilks, K.J., 1992. *Metrication in Australia: A Review of the Effectiveness of Policies and Procedures in Australia's Conversion to the Metric System*, Department of Industry, Technology and Commerce, Australian Government Publishing Service, Canberra. ISBN 0-644-24860-2.

Williams, R., 2012. *The Policy Providers. A History of the Melbourne Institute of Applied Economic and Social Research 1962–2012*, Melbourne University Press, Melbourne.

World Bank, 1994. *Averting the Old Age Crisis: Policies to Protect the Old and Promote Growth*, Oxford University Press, Oxford, UK.

5 The new Millennium

A dispersed labour exchange – the job network[1]

The digital age has made it cheaper and more accurate to detach activities that were previously thought inseparable, such as funding of services from their provision. In 1998, the trickle of outsourced employment services in Australia turned into a torrent.

The decision to undertake a wholesale outsourcing of public services was initially sold to the Australian people as a cost saving measure, but ultimately, it came to be valued for its effect on service quality. Many now argue that the main benefit for jobseekers from Australia's approach to the outsourcing of certain public services comes though bundling the delivery of human services – accommodation, family, employment – into a common provider. The deal is, if the same provider offers them, then the package can be better curated.

From 1946 until 1998, the Commonwealth Employment Service (CES) dominated the provision of employment services.[2] Basic job matching was its primary service, but during the 1990s, the CES extended into training programs, wages subsidies, case management and job creation programs (DEETYA, 1997). However, the CES never held a monopoly. Labour exchanges were operated by trade unions, at least since the 1920s (O'Donnell 2006); the not-for-profit community sector provided employment services in the 1970s; and State governments funded programs, such as the Victorian Government's JobLink program in the 1980s. Furthermore, there have always been private providers operating in niche occupational labour markets, primarily for the benefit of the prospective employers.[3] The extension of public funding into broader employment service, such as case management stepped up in 1994 and involved both the CES and about 300 non-government providers.[4] Permitting the non-government sector to provide public services does not mean that government provision is inferior, but it does not mean it should be shielded from competition either.[5]

DOI: 10.4324/9781003244424-5

From the late 1980s, there had been growing interest within Canberra governmernt circles, in particular among the departmental heads Sandy Hollway and Michael Keating, to find a way to improve how the Commonwealth delivered employment placement services. A real concern was expressed about the churn of jobseekers through training programes without success in landing them a real job.

In 1996, a new Coalition Howard Government, with a predisposition towards choice, contestability and market-based solutions was elected and in 1998 it announced a gear-change in the philosophy towards public services. Members of Parliament, Amanda Vanstone and Tony Abbott believed that a contestable market-based job matching service would improve outcomes for jobseekers. Whereas the Government would fund the employment services, a variety of organisations would deliver the service. These organisations had to first compete for the right to be a provider of services and they would then be funded on how many unemployed job seekers were placed in a job. According to Dockery (1999), although countries overseas had been introducing market-based mechanisms into public services, this change was bold, broad-based and world-leading.

Although a fast, efficient and equitable matching service (including more comprehensive training and employment experience services) is desirable, it does not necessarily follow that governments should subsidise it. A subsidy can be justified if it makes job matches faster on average (efficiency criterion)[6] or promotes the employment prospects of the most disadvantaged job seekers (equity criterion). Under the equity rule, information services may require a subsidy if disadvantaged people do not know or appreciate the value of the information until they have consumed it. Free placement services therefore help promote equal access to jobs regardless of ability to pay. However, its role should not be exaggerated. Public placement services have traditionally been critical in less than 10% of job matches in Australia (ABS cat 6209.0) as most job seekers find matches through personal contacts, advertising platforms or by direct approaches.

Little resistance was mounted to oppose these reforms. According to Wooden and Harding (1998) most employers did not have high expectations of either the CES or recruits attracted by them. Many believed that the CES was mainly interested in shifting people off their books and that the staff did not have the skills to appropriately match people with the sort of jobs on offer (DEETYA 1996, Table 7.4). The work culture of the CES was poor[7] and there was no clear resistance from trade unions to the new scheme, potentially because unions could themselves apply to be a new provider.

The new labour exchange was dubbed the Job Network. Although its promise was to find 'real jobs for all unemployed', there is no evidence that the Job Network reduced the time unemployed people took to find a job.[8]

Nonetheless, there is clear evidence that it reduced the cost of employment services generally as it was contemporaneous with the demolition of the (previous) Labor Government's labour market program structure.

It was hoped that job seekers would value the choice over their employment service provider, but a 2002 Productivity Commission review found that choice was playing a minimal role because of information deficiencies. This review also found that many disadvantaged job seekers receive little assistance while on 'Intensive' Assistance – so-called 'parking' (DEWR, 2002). There were concerns about the complexity and expense of the administrative rules regarding the competitive tendering process. Subsequent reviews by Thomas (2007; O'Flynn, J., 2007) found that these issues remained five years later.

However, the general concept of wholescale outsourced employment service endured. Each successive Australian Government has re-named this exchange (to Job Services Australia in 2009 and the Jobactive program in 2015) but the spirit of the market-based approach has lived on. Following the pattern established in 1994, these services – basic job matching, training, intensive services for the most disadvantaged and work experience – are outsourced through a competitive process to a broad variety of welfare and industry organisations.

Successive economic evaluations have found that the new iteration of the labour exchange network has reduced the time jobseekers take to find work (and or leave welfare payments) but these evaluations are internal to the department. As noted by the 2002 Productivity Commission, the major advantage of this network is the scope given providers to tailor services to their clients' needs and test innovative methods for motivating job seekers and increasing their employability.

A national safety net for people with disabilities – the NDIS[9]

It takes a village to rear a child and a coalition to create a new social innovation. An insurance scheme to provide a service safety net for people with disabilities was first proposed in New Zealand by the Woodhouse Report in 1967. It recommended looking at the needs of the injured rather than the uncertain and expensive route of establishing fault.

It re-appeared in Australia in 1973 as an offshoot of Report of the National Committee of Inquiry into Compensation and Rehabilitation in Australia (Woodhouse and Meares 1974). It sought to address what Prime Minister Whitlam called the 'inequality of luck'. At the time, compensation schemes paid at variable rates with massive gaps so that people with an acquired injury from a traffic accident were supported differently from those born with the same disability or those who developed it through disease. However, best policy dictates that all injuries should be treated equally regardless of origin (congenital, disease or accident). Although universal medical insurance was eventually enacted by Whitlam's Labor Government, the disability element was cancelled following his loss of government in late 1975.

Nevertheless, the idea did not disappear. Behind the scenes, activists John Walsh, an actuary from PWC, and Chris Cuffe continued to agitate for reform. Disability was included in the landmark Social Security Review, 1986–1988, led by Bettina Cass (Cass, Gibson and Tito 1988). Sympathetic social pioneers Bruce Bonyhady, Brian Howe, Bill Shorten, Fiona Tito and Jan McLucas joined the cause (Howe 1989).[10] From the early 2000s, under Presidents Drs Kerryn Phelps, Bill Glasson, Mukesh Haikerwal and Andrew Pesce, the Australian Medical Association had been promoting better care for disabled people. These people understood that the design of effective and efficient disability support needs to begin with a green field. It would be a wasted opportunity to tinker or build on existing foundations. A fresh vision was required.

From the 1990s to 2007, however, there were no government or political leaders taking an interest in the issue and research and community support was sidelined. Public servants' reports were buried, staff budgets were cut, people with knowledge in the area left the Commonwealth department of health and other priorities emerged. The Australian Medical Association was quite happy to see the idea die.

By 2007, disability support – meaning subsidies for wheelchairs and hearing aids, building modification, personal care, specialist accommodation, psychological services and so forth – was operated by an unco-ordinated collage of services across Australia's three-tiered system of government. Programs were ad hoc and there were clear incentives for each tier of government to shift costs on to both other tiers and the larger health and education budgets. The outcomes were inefficient and scarcely in the best interests of people with disabilities. To partly address these shortcomings, a joint Commonwealth/State[11] agreement had been made. However, each State adopted different funding rules leading to inequity of treatment across jurisdictions, type and causes of disability.[12] The States either directly supported care services or dispersed funds to disability organisations who essentially dictated the type of support each person could receive, albeit sometimes after a long wait.

In February 2007, a Senate Community Affairs Legislative Committee[13] was formed to examine alternative funding, jurisdiction and administrative arrangements for disability support. The first issue was to define the problem. Recommendations for more funds without a renewed re-think about the problem was not efficient. The Committee did not recommend an insurance approach to disability support but endorsed a whole of life approach to replace the existing structure of support.

Just before the 2007 November Federal election, John Walsh proposed to Labor Senator Jan McLucas and the then NSW Minister for disability, an insurance-based approach to the delivery of disability services. This idea was subsequently taken up with Ministers and senior members from the new Rudd Labor Government, Jenny Macklin and with Bill Shorten who at the time was the Parliamentary Secretary for Disabilities and Children's Services. Bruce Bonyhady proposed a disability insurance scheme at the New Labor Government's 2020 Summit, but Prime Minister Rudd chose to not take it further at that time.

Undaunted, an alliance of people, determined to change disability support, ploughed on. The challenges facing the team were significant – not the least because the 2008 financial crisis was dominating the airwaves and the minds and souls of business, households and government. To try and introduce a new major budget item at that time was truly audacious.

The team devised a strategy. Bill Shorten, the responsible Parliamentary Secretary, was charged with taking Labor's commitment to a National Disability Strategy forward and constituted a Disability Investment Group to explore opportunities for private investment in disability support. The Group realised that it needed to build community support. Rhonda Galbally launched the 'Shut Out' Report to get public buy in and raise public consciousness. Both reports assisted getting an insurance scheme on the policy agenda with the necessary implications for the budget.

Knowing the importance of getting the 'pointy heads' from central government agencies on board, Jenny Macklin, backed by the advice of her department, lobbied in Cabinet for the Productivity Commission to undertake an Inquiry on the feasibility of a disability insurance scheme in 2009. She was successful and in 2009 Assistant Treasurer Nick Sherry formally commissioned the Productivity Commission to the task. In August 2011 after receiving the Commission's report in July of that year, Labor Prime Minister Julia Gillard announced that the Commonwealth would begin immediate work with states to build the foundations for a National Disability Insurance Scheme (NDIS) (Productivity Commission 2011). The Council of Australian Governments agreed to establish the Ministerial Council on Disability Reform comprising disability Ministers and Treasurers to work together on the NDIS.

Even before the Productivity Commission Report, community organisations were focussed on the task. In 2009, groups such as National Disability Services; Australian Federation of Disability Organisations and Carers Australia devised campaigns to win hearts and minds to this revolutionary idea.

An early milestone was the launch in 2011 of the 'Every Australian Counts' campaign. There were numerous town hall events, members of parliament were lobbied, and an alliance from the disabled community was formed to get them to focus on a common goal, not on their differences. A social marketing campaign was undertaken to create grass roots support and public awareness of the issues. Sympathetic journalists were courted. It was important to disarm, or at least neutralise, antagonistic sceptics and finally, to focus government attention on the unmet needs of people with a disability. The stage was set for serious implementation.[14]

Winning the State Governments, and their public servants, over to the idea took many months and meetings. Part of the additional funds required were drawn from an additional impost on income tax (via the Medicare Levy), which was no mean feat given the tumultuous economic times. This levy proved important in eventually swaying the States.

In 2012, Labor Prime Minister Julia Gillard introduced the National Disability Insurance Scheme Bill into parliament and it was received with bi-partisan support. The scheme is referred to as insurance, as it aimed to 'insure' that all Australian citizens will have costs covered in the event they are born with or acquire a disability (even though it was not based on individual contributions as per normal insurance principles). A key part of the scheme was to give the person, regardless of the origin of the disability, control over how they should be supported. In contrast to past schemes, requests from supportees were often to reduce social isolation and check employment discrimination. Support was no longer just about physical infrastructure.

At the time of establishment, the NDIS had limited international precedents. The UK was giving vouchers directly to the person in need whereas support via the NDIS scheme was brokered through an intermediary, but both types of support aimed to give the person with the disability more control over their lives. The ethos was – what do you want to do with your life? Not, what disability do you have? One of the major innovations of the new scheme was giving participants the capacity to self-manage their support budget if they wish or have it managed for them. Either way the scheme was designed to provide more choice about both the nature of the support relevant to an individual's goals and from where they obtain the resources to achieve those goals.

Australia's national electricity market – the NEM

Australia's National Electricity Market – the NEM – is unique, in the same way that all national electricity markets the world over are unique. Every country has differing topographies and internal governance arrangements. Some countries are governed through unitary structures and some as federations. Some nations operate on continents where the neighbours are friendly, and others operate where the neighbours are not. For all these reasons, and more, a nation's electricity system needs to be able to accommodate these differences if it is to achieve the generally accepted three 'Es' of energy policy: Economic Efficiency, Energy Security and Environmental Sustainability. North America attempts to achieve some of these policy goals by harnessing and sharing some of the energy resources of Canada, the United States of America and Mexico. Some other European nations do the same.

However, there are some characteristics of Australia's NEM that are very different from that seen elsewhere. The NEM is the largest geographical interconnected power system in the world but also with one of the lowest population densities in the OECD (IEA 2005, 2012). It covers approximately 4,500 kilometres, and runs from along Australia's eastern seaboard, from Port Douglas in Far North Queensland to Victoria, across to Tasmania via an undersea link, and to Port Lincoln in South Australia. The NEM does not extend to Western Australia and the Northern Territory, given their significant distances from other centres of the Australian population. Western Australia and the Northern Territory have their own, very different electricity markets that are best suited to their circumstances.

The NEM is an interesting experiment. It is an experiment in cooperative federalism. And it's an experiment in the application of good governance within a complex and rapidly changing market.

By the standards of a number of other Australian institutions, the NEM is still maturing. Prior to the 1990s, electricity was primarily provided by State or Territory governments. In the early 1990s, Victoria began privatising its electricity network, and following the 'Hilmer Review' of Australia's Competition Policy, introduced competition into its electricity generation, distribution and retail networks. In 1996, most of the southern States and Territories of Australia, Queensland, New South Wales, the Australian Capital Territory, Victoria and South Australia decided to enact laws that would support the establishment of a national electricity market for electricity generators, distributors and retailers. And so, in December 1998, the NEM was born.

The National Electricity Market has a sophisticated regulatory regime that provides overall national governance, which separates the rule making, the rules supervision and the operation of the national market. It also has an imaginative approach to competition issues within this complex system that draws on the nation's experience in competition law and at the same time is capable of using the expertise of regulators within the energy system to help inform the community on energy matters.

Importantly, each of Australia's States and Territories have a significant and independent say in how some elements of the NEM operates. In that sense, we should think of the NEM in terms of its physical, interconnected infrastructure, but have an open mind about the way the governance of the NEM operates. We should also think about the NEM as being a triumph in the generally difficult operation of the Australian Federation. In its 2012 review of Australia, the International Energy Agency stated that Australia had one of the most advanced markets for electricity in the OECD (IEA, 2102 p. 89).

When understood, the NEM discloses some very important public policy lessons and innovations. Public policy, particularly policy as important and complex as that which covers a nation's energy supply, operates best when it is constantly under review. The NEM of 2020 is very different from the NEM which was established in 1998. It's different because in a world where renewable energy is becoming the norm, where technology is constantly changing, governments, participants in the system and customers of the system have learned more about the contemporary challenges facing electricity networks, what works and what doesn't, and modifications have been made to the NEM over time based on learning-by-doing within tis highly complex envoronment. From its inception, the NEM has had a number of public reviews including the 2002 Parer Energy Market Review; 2007 Energy Reform: The way forward for Australia; 2015 Energy White Paper; and the 2017 Finkel Review into the Future Security of the National Electricity Market.

Most of the reviews were primarily technical in nature and brought forth some sensible organisational and governance changes based on well-accepted regulatory and public policy principles and, until recently, politically acceptable solutions. However, the politically poisonous issue in Australia of how to reduce carbon emissions has in recent times made effective and timely changes to the operations of the NEM much more difficult.

The NEM from its inception has operated under a consistent and clear set of principles. Although the political process accepts overall governance and accountability for the operation of the NEM, the regulation and the operations of the NEM are independent of the political process and relatively insulated from political interference. The NEM operates as a market, where market-based signals of price and consumer demand are intended to drive public and private investment demand. There are limits nonetheless to the extent to which the market provides optimum outcomes for consumers, and therefore sophisticated, but non-political interventions are sometimes necessary. Addressing perceived market failures demands an equally sophisticated regulatory framework.

Therefore, the operation of the NEM necessitates institutional innovation, and hence a number of independent, market reinforcing institutions have been created. The Australian Energy Market Operator (AEMO) was created to ensure the efficient and safe day-to-day operations of the NEM; the Australian Energy Market Commission (AEMC) was established as the rule maker of the NEM, to diligently ensure that the NEM rules were, and continue to be 'fit for purpose', and to seek agreement to any changes to the NEM rules by the overarching political process, normally the Council of Australian Governments (COAG); the Australian Energy Regulator (AER) was established to apply the NEM rules for the wholesale and retail energy markets and energy networks. Importantly, the NEM is required to conform to appropriate consumer protections specified by the National Energy Consumer Framework (NECF) and very sensibly, these consumer protections are administered by the Australian Consumer and Competition Commission, with input from NEM regulators.

Although these arrangements have served Australia well in the past, they may be inadequate for the future. The current governance arrangements for the NEM are designed for a world where the generator, transmitter and retailer are clearly separate from the consumer. In the energy world of 2020 and beyond, where significant energy is generated by solar and wind, the producer and the consumer and even the wholesaler of solar power for example are often one and the same entity. This applies today in the retail world of householders, and also to some extent in the Australian business world.

It's very interesting to note how the tone of the 2018 IEA report on Australia differs from previous reports, and in particular, the decidedly up-beat 2012 review. *'The energy market and policy environment in Australia have seen rapid changes during the five years since the IEA presented its last in-depth review of Australia in 2012. In line with global energy markets trends, Australia's energy system is undergoing a profound transformation, bringing about challenges in design of energy and climate policies and energy markets'* (IEA 2018, p. 13).

As the IEA appropriately records, these challenges for Australia are, and will remain, profound. It remains to be seen if the current structures within the NEM can survive. Governments have attempted to address some of the challenges alluded to by the IEA with, for example, the establishment in 2017 of the Energy Security Board. The Energy Security Board was originally established to bring some form of coordination to the implementation of the recommendations of the Independent Review into the Future Security of the National Electricity Market. The role of the Energy Security Board *'will also provide whole of system oversight for energy security and reliability to drive better outcomes for consumers'* (COAG Energy Council website, 28 May 2020).

If this is the role of the Energy Security Board, what now then is the contemporary role of the AEMO, and the AER in this regard? In addition, up until now, the NEM has been distinguished by its governance clarity, with each organisation in the NEM's regulatory structure having clear accountability and independent governance arrangements. However, given that the leaders of the Energy Security Board are also the leaders of the AER, the AEMC, and AEMO, where does the prime responsibility for these individuals now lie? Is it with the organisations they lead, or to the Energy Security Board? These are matters that must be resolved for the long-term health of the NEM.

Another important and related matter that the NEM regulators, in conjunction with the COAG Energy Council must urgently resolve is how to communicate about demand and supply issues within the NEM to what is now a highly diverse producer and customer base, and where State and Territory Governments feel an obligation to meet the clean energy demands of their constituents by encouraging State based clean energy initiatives, independent of national energy policies.

The information requirements of the current electricity consumer and producer base in a possible post carbon world is highly complex. If individual householders and non-energy related firms are to remain, or increase their direct involvement in the construction, supply and reliability of the NEM, then they will need to be communicated with so as to help them to make important investment decisions in the future. Should they extend, or replace their existing roof-top solar systems? Should they invest in battery technology that could be used as back up for the grid for when the sun doesn't shine, and the wind doesn't blow? What is likely to be their return on investment? In its current form, is the NEM and its current regulatory structure capable of meeting these critical contemporary challenges?

The NEM is an important Australian public policy innovation. The quality of its past performance is well recognised. However, the challenge now facing the NEM is to adjust to a more complex set of challenges than those that applied when it was established in 1998.

If it can do that, then it will truly be a great Australian innovation.

A comprehensive business panel dataset – BLADE[15]

The Business Analysis Longitudinal Data Environment was born in the back of a taxi. Although there had been three prior attempts at the Australia Bureau of Statistics (ABS) to build a business panel dataset, the final, ultimately successful initiative to create a comprehensive business panel database took off in early 2013 after a meeting between two ABS employees, Diane Braskic and Helen Teasdale, and the Victorian State Government.

Panel data are repeat observations on the same unit over successive time periods. In industrial economics, a panel dataset will consist of annual observations, on say, sales, employment and exports, from the same business. Panel datasets are valued in research as it allows the analyst to statistically control for confounding but unmeasured features of the firm, such as managerial quality or the market niche of the firm. If analysts can control for these unmeasured features, they have greater confidence about the causal role of the measured factors (such as participation in a government program or spending on R&D). Furthermore, our statistical techniques allow us to quantify the importance of these amorphic, unmeasured features. Business longitudinal databases give a more nuanced window on the behaviour of markets: Is growth driven by a few champions or the median firm? Are there high entry and exit rates from the market, or is it very stable?

Such is the power of panel data analysis, that it is now the standard international benchmark for program evaluation, causal inference and even descriptive analysis.

Let us be clear about the stakes: the Australian Government, let alone the State and Local Governments, spend over $10 billion a year on programs to improve the productivity of Australian business, either through encouraging innovation, improving management and smoothing the way for export penetration *inter alia*. Without rigorous scrutiny of this expenditure, we could be wasting money and depriving other areas of public need – transport, education and health – of vital funds.

Datasets permit objective and scientific evaluation of business activities and the analysis of Australian research, innovation and productivity. They are therefore a foundation for improved public policy. However, such datasets do not materialise on their own. It takes a consortium of people with the same vision and determination to, first, create these research tools, and then, to persist until the instrument achieves its own momentum.

The vision for an Australian business panel dataset began before the early 1990s when it was apparent that Australian business data not only lagged other datasets in the social sciences but also business databases elsewhere in the world (e.g. the U.S. has had a business panel since 1975, Adams and Peck 1994, McGuckin and Pascoe 1988).

In response to a funded request from the Office of Small Business, Bill Pattinson from the ABS ran the Business Longitudinal Survey from 1994–1995 to 1997–1998 (Hawke 2000). Although the survey covered a rich variety of fields (from a sample of 13,000 firms), the short length of the panel and the categorical variables resulted in modest uptake by researchers in academic and government (especially the Bureau of Industry Economics and the Productivity Commission) and it was abandoned after four waves (Will and Wilson 2001). The second attempt in 2004 was undertaken by Murray Klee and Geoff Heffernan from the ABS and Beth Webster, Alfons Palangkaraya and Paul Jensen from the University of Melbourne and involved linking business units within the pre-existing Manufacturing Census. This resulted in three papers, but a lack of resources within the ABS led to the dataset being deleted and the end of the research program.[16] Finally, in 2005, the ABS was funded by the Australian Government to conduct another survey based on about 10,000 businesses. However, its small sample size meant it had limited application at the granular level and it was not suitable for program evaluation.

In the meantime, the same economists at the University of Melbourne, Ben Mitra-Kahn from IP Australia, and Mark Cully and Louise Talbot from the Australian department of industry had been lobbying by letter and in committees for the ABS to link its internal tax, survey and administrative records to produce a business panel dataset for researchers. The introduction of the GST in 2001 and the subsequent creation of a unique Australian Business Number, opened up an opportunity to link administrative data and thereby provide a cheap and comprehensive substitute for expensive sample survey data.

Hence in early 2013, Diane Braskic and Helen Teasdale met with these University of Melbourne economists and began a project to link the Business Income Tax and Business Activity Statement data under the romantic nomenclature of the 'BAS-BIT' dataset. In partnership with the Victorian Government's department of industry,[17] the aim was to use the population characteristic of the BAS-BIT to evaluate one of the Government's business programs. The BAS-BIT contained 1.5 million firms and 12 years of data. The project was given a boost in 2014 when the Chief Economist of the Commonwealth Department of Industry, Mark Cully, aided by Luke Hendrickson, also from the same Department, made substantial funds available to extend the database and place it on a more secure footing (Hansell and Rafi 2018). It was further supported with the appointment of David Kalish as the ABS Chief Statistician in late 2014. David immediately saw its enormous potential. The database was renamed even more torturously as the EABLD and then, fortunately by a better anagramologist, as BLADE.

The greater coverage of the dataset, and its ability to use historic information to create an instant panel of about eight years, meant it quickly gained traction among users. This (latent) demand was critical to its longevity, for this breadth of support was critical for achieving program priority within influential circles.

Access to the data has been a major pain point for both users and providers of BLADE. Negotiating around the very tight access restrictions for outside researchers took many years. The data is now de-identified and confidential, and the ABS is required to adopt processes to remove even a small chance of a data breach. However, without significant use of the data by relevant parties, support to continue the dataset will not be forthcoming.

The sustainability of BLADE depended critically on usage and visible value for Governments. A number of department of industry and Swinburne research papers using BLADE from 2015 onwards was important, in government circles at least, in putting significant pressure on the ABS to substantially improve their commitment to BLADE via the Data Integration Partnership for Australia program (e.g. Hendrickson, Bucifal, Balaguer and Hansell 2015; Tuhin and Swanepoel 2016; Palangkaraya and Webster 2015).

Hence, the next wave of innovation was to smooth the path of access while maintaining the integrity of confidentiality. Initially, users had to submit command files to the ABS who would then run the program and check the output before release. The difficulty of blind interrogation of the data meant that a straightforward research paper could take up to four years to complete. Subsequently, the ABS introduced the 5-safes process for the treatment of confidential data and access was gradually enhanced for approved researchers and research projects. By 2019, changes to ABS legislation had made access to BLADE from the desktop or via a data laboratory possible for a broader range of researchers.

Parallel with this has been increased integration of more data into BLADE and a formal structure set up within the Australian Department of Prime Minister and Cabinet to fund and vet projects. It is now (2020) considered a major tool with over 1,000 registered users from over six government agencies and universities.

Evidence to understand household behaviours – HILDA[18]

It took a frustrated economic modeler, a favourable politician and a fanatical academic to create a world-leading household panel dataset.

Knowing why some people drop out of education and training; why people do not save for retirement; estimating the effect of parental poverty on child outcomes and tracing the long-term effects of unemployment should be based on more than just anecdote and guesswork. Eradicating these socio-economic ills with better targeted policy is one of the key goals of any good government.

Not all data are equal however. Inferring causation from cross-sectional data is not robust as correlations may represent reverse causation or a third confounding factor. Panel data, which combines cross-sectional data over multiple time periods, allows greater leverage on questions of causality, as well as providing information on individual trajectories. The road to ineffectual policy is paved with good intentions, but nothing beats objective evidence for demolishing myths and replacing bad with good policy.

However, collecting panel data is expensive, not least because you must track the same person or household over long periods of time. It is remarkable then that the USA began their ongoing person panel data collection – the Panel Study of Income Dynamics (PSID) – in 1968.

By the late 1990s, computer-based surveys were becoming standard practise and the costs of data collection had fallen considerably. Ken Oliver from the Australian social security department,[19] had become increasingly dispirited by the poor quality of parameters for his microsimulation models. He was aware of the data from the PSID and started to a campaign for an

Australian version from within the Department. Chris Foster and Wayne Jackson, the 2IC at the time, instantly saw its potential and championed the project within the bureaucracy, winning support from the Prime Minister's department and Treasury. The survey was to be both representative of the whole Australian population, and large enough to sustain reasonable levels of disaggregation (by state, sex, education level etc.). The Liberal Treasurer at the time, Peter Costello, supported the idea and despite objections from the department of finance, funding was approved by Cabinet. As luck would have it, the Department was relatively flush with funds that year (1999).

Initially the Australian Bureau of Statistics was approached to run the survey, but the Chief Statistician was unwilling to be involved as he thought biases in the data from selection and attrition would render the dataset below an acceptable standard. And so, the Department issued an open tender, with Meredith Baker baptising the survey, HILDA – the Household, Income and Labour Dynamics in Australia survey.

The Director of the Melbourne Institute of Applied Economic and Social Research (University of Melbourne), Professor Peter Dawkins, seized this opportunity. Building on the Melbourne Institute's reputation for applied economic research, he hired Professor Mark Wooden from Flinders University to lead a consortium of empirical social scientists to develop a convincing proposal a proposal. This was to be no off-the-cuff proposal and involved an intensive two-month effort from Mark Wooden. Wooden trawled the literature to understand what other jurisdictions had done to ensure what he was proposing would be beyond the frontier for best-practice.

The Melbourne Institute bid to conduct the HILDA survey was successful and in 2000 Karen Wilson from the Department took over project management. Concurrently, the Melbourne Institute hired survey-analyst Nicole Watson and took its first steps to develop and deliver the survey for an initial five years. To ensure the team used the best available methods, James Jordan from the Department insisted Wooden visited premier household panel data operations overseas. According to Wooden, James' call was pivotal because the information he gathered and the contacts he built, particularly in the UK and Germany, had a lasting legacy.

The initial proposal contained no provision for financial incentives for participation. But after response rates for the dress rehearsals were poor, James Jordan found extra funding to add financial incentive for participants.

Wooden understood that take-up and use by the research and policy community was the key to ensuring re-funding and the longevity of the survey. A high take-up was not just about ensuring that the questions were unambiguous, tested, internationally standardised and suitable for economic modelling, but also that the databases were well-published and easy for researchers to access. The policy of free, open and supported access to the data was, at the time in contrast to the relative costs and difficulty of using unit record files from other agencies. The Melbourne Institute had a deliberate policy to generate a broad ecosystem of users – academic, community and government. By 2020, there were about 3,600 licensed users of HILDA Survey.

Long-term funding of HILDA has never been assured and every five years a new tranche of funding for HILDA must be passed by the Cabinet. The survey nearly foundered in the early years because of poor funding but was saved by David Gruen (head of Research at the Reserve Bank Australia at the time, and since 2019 head of the Australian Bureau of Statistics), Guy Debelle and Luci Ellis. Very early in the piece, Wooden was making presentations around the country on the proposed operation of HILDA.

At the time of writing (2020), HILDA has produced 1,200 papers and books and contributed to many policy changes. There is no doubt its enduring success is due to the detailed design and management of Mark Wooden who ensured at every step that the operation was world best practice. HILDA also had a subtler effect on the Australian policy landscape. Its success had changed the views of the bureaucracy, especially public-sector data custodians, about the optimal balance between privacy and data access. It has revealed the value that can be obtained from linked data unit records and how safely provisions can work. It moved the default position from 'no' to 'yes'.

Many lucky steps conspired towards the success of HILDA but according to senior Canberra bureaucrat Serena Wilson, 'good change only happens where political opportunity meets prior preparation'.

Notes

1 Grateful thanks to Sandy Hollway for comments on the draft.
2 Free public provision of job matching services has become an ILO obligation under R83 Employment Service Recommendation, 1948.
3 Private agencies have no obligation to find or act on behalf of any interested job seeker and accordingly give selective assistance to job seekers (Boreham, Roan and Whitehouse 1994). Over half of private agency job seekers are already in employment (ABS cat. 6245.0).
4 DEETYA (1996).
5 If government services are superior, then it begs the question of why there is a need to eliminate their competition. Governments may, however, choose to retain monopoly provision in areas where they do not believe they are able to closely assess what the provider is doing and whether they are acting in the public interest.
6 Strictly speaking, the benefits of a faster match must outweigh the extra costs of this service.
7 Contracting out in many cases has thus been employed as a device for quick wholesale reform of public sector work practices.
8 PC (2002).

9   Thanks to Serena Wilson, Jan McLucas, Fiona Tito Wheatland and Pamela Burton for comments on the draft and interviews.
10 Assisted by public servants, led by Serena Wilson, whose role was to take forward policy work from the time of commissioning the Productivity Commission through to the legislation.
11 All states signed onto the National Disability Agreement.
12 Each State had different rules about whether road accident insurance was no fault or not; whether eligibility depended on whether the source of disability was congenital or from accident; whether the accident needed to be work or transport related and so on.
13 The inquiry was called the 'Funding and Operation of the Commonwealth State/ Territory Disability Agreement'.
14 The Group was sceptical about the ability of the Productivity Commission to support the idea and so John Walsh was appointed Assistant Commissioner to the Report and a Reference Group was appointed from the disability sector.
15 Grateful thanks to Diane Braskic, Mark Cully, Dennis Trewin.
16 Leahy, Palangkaraya and Yong (2010); Palangkaraya and Yong (2011a,2011b)
17 Helen Silver, Howard Ronaldson, Matthew Dummett, Tim Kovess, Verena Engbarth, Nicole Mizen.
18 Thanks to Ken Oliver, Mark Wooden, Meredith Baker.
19 The then Commonwealth Department of Families, Housing, Community Services and Indigenous Affairs.

References

Adams, James D. and Peck, Suzanne, 1994. *A Guide to R&D Data at the Center for Economic Studies U.S. Bureau of the Census*, Working Papers 94–9, Center for Economic Studies, Washington, DC: U.S. Census Bureau.

Australia Bureau of Statistics, 2000. *Business Longitudinal Survey Confidentialised Unit Record File (8141.0.30.001)*, 12 June 2000, Canberra: ABS.

Boreham, P., Roan, A. and Whitehouse, G., 1994. The regulation of employment services: Private employment agencies and labour market policy. *Australian Journal of Political Science*, 29(3), pp. 541–555.

Cass, Bettina, Francis Gibson and Fiona Tito, 1988. *Towards Enabling Policies: Income Support for People with Disabilities*, Issues Paper (Social Security Review (Australia)) No. 5, Australian Government Publishing Service, Canberra.

DEETYA, 1996. *Working Nation: Evaluation of the Employment, Educational Training Elements*. Evaluation and Monitoring Branch. EMB Report 2/96, Canberra: Department Education, Employment, Training and Youth Affairs.

DEETYA, 1997. *The Net Impact of Labour Market Programs*, Evaluation and Monitoring Branch, EMB Report 2/97, Canberra: Department Education, Employment, Training and Youth Affairs.

DEWR, 2002. *Job Network Evaluation. Stage Three: Effectiveness Report*, Evaluation and Programme Performance Branch, Labour Market Policy Group, Department of Employment and Workplace Relations, May 2002, Canberra: Department Employment, and Workplace Relations.

Dockery, A.M., 1999. Evaluating the Job Network. *Australian Journal of Labour Economics*, 3(2), p. 131.

Hansell, D. and Rafi, B., 2018. Firm-Level Analysis Using the ABS'Business Longitudinal Analysis Data Environment (BLADE). *Australian Economic Review*, 51(1), pp. 132–138.

Hawke, A., 2000. The Business Longitudinal Survey. *Australian Economic Review*, 33(1), pp. 94–94.

Hendrickson, Luke, Bucifal, Stan, Balaguer, Antonio and Hansell, David, 2015. *The Employment Dynamics of Australian Entrepreneurship*, Canberra: Department of Industry and Science (Office of the Chief Scientist) and Australian Bureau of Statistics, Research Paper 4/2015

Howe, Brian, 1989. *Reforming Income Support for the Unemployed: Report on Public Submissions (and Government Policy Initiatives) in Response to Social Security Review Issues Paper No. 4*, Income Support for the Unemployed in Australia: Towards a More Active System, Commonwealth of Australia, Canberra.

International Energy Agency, 2005. *Energy Policies of IEA Countries, Australia 2005 Review*, OECD/IEA 2005, Paris.

International Energy Agency, 2012. *Energy Policies of IEA Countries, Australia 2012 Review*, OECD/IEA 2012, Paris.

International Energy Agency, 2018. *Energy Policies of IEA Countries, Australia 2018 Review*, OECD/IEA 2018, Paris.

Leahy, A., Palangkaraya, A. and Yong, J., 2010. Geographical Agglomeration in Australian Manufacturing. *Regional Studies*, 44(3), pp. 299–314.

McGuckin, Robert H. and Pascoe, George A., 1988. *The Longitudinal Research Database (LRD): Status and Research Possibilities*, Working Papers 88–2, Center for Economic Studies, Washington DC: U.S. Census Bureau.

O'Donnell, A., 2006. Re-inventing Unemployment: Welfare Reform as Labour Market Regulation. *University of Melbourne Legal Studies Research Paper*, 137, Melbourne: University of Melbourne.

O'Flynn, J., 2007. *Measuring Performance in Australia's Job Network (B), University of Canberra, for Professor John Alford*, Australia and New Zealand School of Government, for Teaching Purposes and to Accompany Cases 2007–37, Melbourne: ANZOG.

Palangkaraya, A. and Webster, E., 2015. *Measuring R&D Spillovers from Australia Industry: Uses and Limitations of Using the Extended Analytic Business Longitudinal Database (EABLD)*, Hawthorn: Centre for Transformative Innovation, Swinburne University of Technology.

Palangkaraya, A. and Yong, J., 2011a. Trade Liberalisation, Exit, and Output and Employment Adjustments of Australian Manufacturing Establishments. *The World Economy*, 34(1), pp. 1–22.

Palangkaraya, A. and Yong, J., 2011b. *Exporter and Non-Exporter Productivity Differentials: Evidence from Australian Manufacturing Establishments*, Melbourne Institute of Applied Economic and Social Research, Melbourne: The University of Melbourne.

Productivity Commission 2002. *Independent Review of the Job Network*, Report No. 21, AusInfo, Canberra.

Productivity Commission, 2011. *Disability Care and Support*, Report No. 54, Canberra, www.pc.gov.au/projects/inquiry/disability-support/report.

Thomas, M., 2007. *A Review of Developments in the Job Network*, Research Paper Index, Research Paper no. 15 2007–08, A Review of Developments in the Job Network, Social Policy Section, 24 December 2007, Canberra: Parliament of Australia.

Tuhin, Razib and Swanepoel, Jan A., 2016. *Export Behaviour and Business Performance: Evidence from Australian Microdata Research*, Department of Industry and Science (Office of the Chief Scientist), Research Paper 7/2016, Canberra: Department of Industry and Science.

Webster, E.M., Harding, D. and Harding, G., 1998. *The Contestability of Publicly Funded Employment and Benefit Services: The Australian Experience*, Report for the New Zealand Treasury, Melbourne Institute of Applied Economic and Social Research, Melbourne: University of Melbourne.

Will, L. and Wilson, H.D., 2001, *Tricks and Traps of the Business Longitudinal Survey*, Melbourne: Productivity Commission Melbourne.

Wooden, M. and Harding, D., 1998. Recruitment Practices in the Private Sector: Results from a National Survey of Employers. *Asia Pacific Journal of Human Resources*, 36(2).

Woodhouse, Arthur and Meares, Charles, 1974. *Compensation and Rehabilitation in Australia: Report of the National Committee of Inquiry*, 3 vols., National Committee of Inquiry on Compensation and Rehabilitation in Australia, Australian Government Publishing Service, Canberra.

6 Conclusion

There is much to learn from this sample of successful Australian economic innovations. The first lesson is that there are always serious economic challenges that demand innovative solutions. This sample of Australian economic innovations show that whatever the time, and whatever the circumstances there are people and organisations that demand our attention if nations like Australia are to make the best use of their human, social and economic endowments.

Australia does not need to look far to understand its significant current economic and social challenges. Coping with a zero net-carbon world will demand economic, social, engineering and political innovation.

Australia's challenge of coping with and supporting an ageing population will test its policy and economic ingenuity. It will demand Australia making the very best use of the declining proportion of its population that is of working age. It will demand that Australia find carers outside of its domestic Australian workforce to support ageing Australians.

Australia's education system is at the crossroads. Although Australia has much to be proud of in relation to its education system, its schools, its vocational education system and its universities, Australia's global leadership in this area is being challenged. An affective innovation system demands an excellent education system.

Coping with the significant aftermath of the COVID-19 crisis and whatever might follow is an existential challenge facing not only Australia but many other nations. For Australia it means rediscovering what it means to be a federated nation, where cooperation between States, Territories and the Federal Government is the norm, not the exception. It also means that Australian governments, State, Territory and the Commonwealth will need to repair their balance sheets so that they are able to cope with the inevitable next global financial challenge. Australia has significantly benefited from cooperative, competitive federalism, and this successful formula for economic growth has been sorely tested by COVID-19 and its aftermath.

DOI: 10.4324/9781003244424-6

COVID-19 has also shown both the importance of Australia being part of a global economic, political and social network, and also the limits of that international system. Australia must not turn its back on the importance of international and free trade. Australia cannot produce all the goods and services that its people demand. Australia must be part of the international trading system, and this will demand that Australian industry has the productivity levels and innovation capability to take its rightful place in that international trading system.

All these challenges will only be met, however, if Australia has the political and community courage and willingness to face up to and tackle these challenges. These few examples of Australian economic innovations have a number of characteristics in common. They all required dedicated individuals who could see and understand the challenges facing them and had the courage to do something about them, often in the face of significant opposition. It required courageous politicians who were prepared to publicly argue the case for reform, often over many years and do something practically about it, again, often in the face of significant opposition. It required politicians to sometimes 'reach across the isle' to seek support from their political opponents, and it required political foes to be sufficiently courageous to accept that the public interest demanded that they put aside their political differences for the benefit of all Australians.

Importantly, these few examples of Australian economic innovations proves that Australia has a proud history of reform, a proud history from which today's reformers and policy makers should take inspiration.

Index

Printed in the United States
by Baker & Taylor Publisher Services